THE
MUNSTER
REPUBLIC

MICHAEL HARRINGTON

THE MUNSTER REPUBLIC

THE CIVIL WAR
IN NORTH CORK

MERCIER PRESS
IRISH PUBLISHER – IRISH STORY

MERCIER PRESS
Cork
www.mercierpress.ie

Trade enquiries to CMD BookSource,
55a Spruce Avenue, Stillorgan Industrial Park,
Blackrock, County Dublin

© Michael Harrington, 2009

ISBN: 978 1 85635 656 5

10 9 8 7 6 5 4 3 2 1

A CIP record for this title is available from the British Library

Do Mháire

Printed and bound in the EU.

Contents

Acknowledgements

I would not have been able to complete this book – which started out as a thesis – without the assistance and support given to me by the institutions, libraries and individuals mentioned below.

I wish to thank Dr Michael Cosgrave for the help and guidance he gave me over the two years it took to research and write this work.

Special thanks are due to the staff of the Military Archives, Cathal Brugha Barracks, for their courtesy and help in my many visits there, particularly Commandant Victor Laing and Commandant Liam Campbell for their comments on the military aspects of the book and, of course, the ever-helpful Alan. The information gleaned from sources in the Military Archives was crucial to completing the work.

My thanks are also due to the staff of the Archives Department, University College, Dublin, for their guidance in researching the Mulcahy papers and the O'Malley documents.

The staff of the Boole Library, University College, Cork (UCC), facilitated me in every way, and I am also indebted to the staff in UCC Special Collections, Pouladuff Road, Cork. Their unfailing patience and guidance was invaluable.

I am grateful to the staff in the Cork Archives Institute for their professionalism and good humour whilst working under difficult conditions in South Main Street in Cork.

The staff of Cork County Library, Model Farm Road, Cork, were always extremely helpful and provided microfilms and readers with a minimum of fuss.

I also wish to thank Michael Byrnes of Charleville for allowing me access to the Motherway papers and for giving me permission to include them in this work.

Finally, thank you Tadhg and Tom for your help and advice in shaping and ordering my writing, and for proofreading the work as it developed.

Abbreviations

The following abbreviations are used in the text and in the references:

ASU	Active Service Unit
CAI	Cork Archives Institute
CCL	Cork County Library
CIC	Commander-in-Chief
DCS	Deputy Chief-of-Staff
FS	Free State
GHQ	General Headquarters
HQ	Headquarters
I/O	Intelligence Officer
L gun	Lewis gun
M/A	Military Archives (Cathal Brugha Barracks, Dublin)
M/P	Mulcahy papers
O/C	Officer Commanding
PG	Provisional Government
RIC	Royal Irish Constabulary
TD	Teachta Dála (Member of the Dáil)
T gun	Thompson (Tommy) gun
UCC	University College, Cork
UCD	University College, Dublin
WS	Witness Statement

Glossary of Terms

Republicans	Anti-Treaty forces
Irregulars	Anti-Treaty forces as referred to by the Free State government
Staters	Forces of the Free State
Executive Forces	Republicans or anti-Treaty forces operating under the aegis of the Volunteer executive post-March 1922.
Provisional Government	Pro-Treaty government up to 6 December 1922
Free State Government	Pro-Treaty government after 6 December 1922
Newtown/ Newtownshandrum	Newtown and Newtownshandrum in the text are the same place. The village is officially called Newtown, but Shandrum, the name of the parish in which it is situated, is often added to distinguish it from other Newtowns.

Prologue
The End of the War of Independence in North Cork

The implications of the King's Speech at the opening of the Parliament of Northern Ireland on 22 June 1921, in which he appealed to all Irishmen 'to pause, to stretch out the hand of forbearance and conciliation, to forgive and forget',[1] were lost on the Volunteers fighting in the field in North Cork in late June and early July 1922. Neither would they have read much of significance into the release of de Valera from custody on 23 June, or Lloyd George's appeal to de Valera to meet him and James Craig in London 'to end the ruinous conflict that has for centuries divided Ireland, and embittered the relations of the peoples of these two islands'.[2] It is doubtful that they would have 'cheered [General Sir Nevil] Macready to his meeting with the Irish leaders, to discuss truce terms, at the Mansion House on July 8th', as did the delighted crowds in Dublin.[3] These were young fighting men who had spent two years on the run from British forces. They were wanted men whose lives were forfeit if they were captured in possession of arms. Their sole focus was on ambushing British forces whenever the opportunity presented itself, as outlined by Paddy O'Brien, commandant of Cork No. 4 brigade, as follows:

> We got an invitation from West Limerick with a view to bringing off some action on a large scale between Newcastlewest and Abbeyfeale. I directed a number of our men to immediately start making about eight mines filled with about 14 lbs of explosive. The column leader in Newmarket, Michael D. O'Sullivan, and myself went into

11

the West Limerick area and met some of the Abbeyfeale battalion at Tournafulla. They informed us that there was a convoy of military passing regularly each week between Newcastlewest and Abbeyfeale. We chose a position between Ardagh and Templeglantine where we could get reasonably good fire positions, ranging from between thirty to one hundred yards.

On the night of July 7th a column of eighty men from North Cork proceeded by Rockchapel to the vicinity of Tournafulla where we met the West Limerick column of about sixty men. The following morning we had eight mines placed in the road enclosing a distance of nearly a mile. The columns were divided into sections covering each of the eight positions and allowing for protection on the flanks. Four lorries were observed coming and we decided to attack them on the return journey. They returned by another route to Newcastlewest. It was decided to wait until the following Monday when the convoy would again be likely to pass.

Late on Saturday evening, July 9th, a dispatch arrived from divisional headquarters summoning myself and the battalion O/Cs, who were with the column to a meeting at Dromahane on Sunday, July 10th. It was then that we were definitely informed that there was to be a truce the following day at noon. I then asked if it would be permissible for the column to carry out an attack on the following morning and was informed by the divisional O/C that we could please ourselves. We returned to Tournafulla that night and held a conference with the section leaders of North Cork and the officers of the West Limerick column. It was unanimously decided that we would go back to the positions evacuated on Friday and remain there until 12 noon. The column was dismissed at 12 noon and at 12.15 p.m., when the men were actually removing some of the mines from the road, a military party came on the scene from Newcastlewest. These, seeing our men on the road, first attempted to be hostile, but when asked if they were prepared to observe the Truce they changed their manner and continued on their way to Abbeyfeale.[4]

This is how the War of Independence concluded in the area of operations of Cork No. 4 brigade. This was a well-planned operation and could have been catastrophic for the British forces, possibly eclipsing Tom Barry's Kilmichael ambush. In the account of Commandant Paddy O'Brien, there is a sense of disappointment and frustration among the Volunteers at not engaging the British forces. Their two-week preparations for a large-scale ambush show they were unaware that a truce was imminent. Their chagrin at the ambush being aborted is at variance with the mood of the editorial of the *Cork Examiner* of 11 July, which stated that 'congratulations and jubilation and increased hopefulness represent the Irish mood today' as a result of the commencement of the Truce. These men were ill-prepared for the adulation shortly to be directed at them and for the compromises that might be necessary. Like Liam Lynch, they 'declared for an Irish Republic', and were not prepared to 'live under any other law'.[5]

Introduction

It could be argued that the Civil War was one of the greatest disasters in Irish history and yet, paradoxically, it may have copper-fastened Irish democracy. All other Irish wars were fought against Britain, a country perceived to have colonised Ireland at the time of the Norman invasion of 1169 and to have subsequently controlled Ireland by use of force.

It is ironic that, having forced the traditional enemy to come to the negotiating table through the War of Independence, Volunteers who had fought in common cause should then turn on each other, ostensibly over the negotiated settlement, in a savage internecine war. It is equally ironic that the Civil War protagonists spawned two political parties based solely on the opposing factions in that war, and that from the birth of these parties to this day, all issues, local and national, have been dealt with in an exemplary democratic fashion, and that successive transfers of governmental power have occurred without difficulty.

Seeking to discern the causes of the Civil War often prompts a partisan approach, invites dissension and can descend into apportioning blame. The Civil War did not happen overnight – it was at least one full year in gestation. None of the principal protagonists wanted to fire the first shot and many strove might and main to avoid an outbreak of large-scale fighting. It can even be argued that strenuous efforts by both sides to unify the IRA and generous gestures by opposing leaders to defuse flash-points were factors in the eventual republican (anti-Treaty) defeat. At any rate, it is timely to revisit that sad period in Irish history now that the principal protagonists have passed on and much of the hurt has been assuaged by the kind passage of time.

Éamon de Valera was the pre-eminent Irish leader at the time of the War of Independence and the Civil War. He was president of Dáil Éireann, the Volunteers and Sinn Féin. The role of de Valera in the lead-up to the Civil War must be examined. Was he a leader intoxicated by his own status and someone who firmly believed that his perception of events transcended the views of others? Was he machiavellian in his planning, orchestrating the elimination of rivals through the negotiating process with Britain? Or was he a leader with supreme insight – one who saw conflict arising out of intractable positions taken up by people with sincerely held but diametrically opposed views? The case can be made that he was a highly perceptive politician who wrestled intellectually with the problems thrown up by the London negotiations and who produced a brilliant compromise approach – external association – which he believed had the potential to satisfy all, Britain included. Equally, important was the role played by British prime minister, David Lloyd George. Did he reject de Valera's brainchild of external association because of his inability to appreciate its nuances and his failure to recognise Irish difficulties in negotiating a treaty that could command widespread acceptance across the Irish political spectrum? Consequently, did his actions precipitate Ireland's Civil War?

When the Civil War finally began, it seemed that the republicans had the advantage, at least on paper. They were dominant in Dublin and controlled most of the provinces of Munster, Connacht and Ulster. Their leaders were the heroes of many War of Independence engagements, their soldiers were veterans, they held sway in the majority of provincial towns and they had a plentiful supply of arms. If they moved on the capital in force, Dublin was at their mercy. Yet within two months of the outbreak of the war, Provisional Government forces controlled the towns and cities countrywide, and the republicans had become a guerrilla army. Possible reasons for the republican collapse need to be examined at national and local level.

As a guerrilla force, the republicans were more successful in some areas than others. In the autumn and winter of 1922, for instance, Cork No. 4 brigade dominated the countryside in North Cork, while in much of Cork county and city, the Free State forces held sway. The major part of this book examines the fighting between the Free State forces and the republicans in the battles for Limerick and Kilmallock, and especially the conflict between Free State forces and Cork No. 4 brigade in North Cork.

Writing objective accounts of the Civil War has been notoriously difficult, partly because the war never ended formally – it simply petered out. The republicans never formally surrendered, no compromise was achieved and, as a result, reconciliation between protagonists at local and national level never happened. While participants in the War of Independence willingly gave full accounts of their activities in many forms to writers and to the Military Archives, few survivors of the Civil War, especially on the republican side, committed their accounts to paper. As a result, it has been difficult to access primary sources so as to do justice to both sides of the conflict. Recently released files of the Civil War operations of the Free State forces – now housed in the Military Archives – contain many captured republican documents. These files, in conjunction with the Mulcahy papers and the O'Malley papers and notebooks, provide most of the primary sources for writing on the Civil War.

If the Civil War had a positive outcome, it is that the Irish people in the Republic never again resorted to conflict to resolve intractable issues, and that democracy has been unquestionably accepted as the system of government of the people.

1
Build-up to the Civil War

THE TRUCE NEGOTIATIONS

Éamon de Valera was acknowledged as the primary Irish nationalist leader in June 1921. He was the senior surviving commandant of the 1916 Rising, but escaped execution because his 'death sentence was commuted in deference to his American nationality'.[1] However, he was interned for his involvement in the Rising, serving his sentence in England, and 'at Dartmoor and Lewes de Valera's quality of leadership asserted itself'.[2] The internees were released in 1917 and welcomed on the streets of Dublin by huge crowds. Younger notes that 'de Valera was singled out for special adulation'.[3] De Valera's rise to power was dramatic, and potential leaders of Sinn Féin were 'quickly eclipsed by the new star, Éamon de Valera, who had no intention of brooking any rivals for the leadership after his release'.[4] The aura of a 1916 leader and the emotional force generated by the executions of the main protagonists was embodied in Sinn Féin when 'de Valera was unanimously elected president of both Sinn Féin and the Irish Volunteers in October 1917 thus blurring the differences between the political and the paramilitary movements'.[5] This resulted in the leadership of the political and military movements being invested in one person, with consequent immense power, control and responsibility. Moreover, de Valera was elected president of the Dáil on 1 April 1921, and was able to chose who would become government ministers.[6] This presidency of the Dáil further added to de Valera's prestige and power.

In keeping with his high-profile position, de Valera took 'immediate personal control of the negotiations when the Anglo-Irish Truce, bringing an end to the war, was signed on 11 July 1921'.[7] J.M. Curran explains that 'de Valera was eager to discuss peace. He knew that Sinn Féin could not force Britain to recognise a completely independent Republic and that this demand also impeded Irish unification.'[8] De Valera was now 'back in the position he had taken up in 1917 – the conciliator in nationalist ranks, the political strategist and diplomat who would, hopefully, unite all elements within the Dáil cabinet' and, above all, 'find a formula to accommodate Irish republicanism to the prospect of necessary compromise'.[9]

De Valera made several attempts to warn all parties that such an all-encompassing formula entailed compromise. Lee states that de Valera warned the Dáil in August 1921 – as bluntly as was politically possible – that compromise was inevitable. He quotes de Valera stressing that he took office again as president only on condition that the Dáil recognised that:

> I have one allegiance only to the people of Ireland, and that is to do the best we can for the people of Ireland as we conceive it ... I would not like, therefore, that anyone should propose me for election as president who would think I had my mind definitely made up on any situation that may arise. I keep myself free to consider each question as it arises – I never bind myself in any other way.[10]

While speaking to the Dáil, de Valera was also indirectly addressing the diehard republican constituency. Lee makes it clear that 'this came as close as de Valera could safely go in implying that the oath to the Republic taken by members should be considered more a means to an end than an end in itself'.[11] Speaking to the Dáil on 16 August in relation to the mandate Sinn Féin had received at the 1918 election, de Valera stated: 'I do not say that answer was for a form of government so much, because we are not republican doctrinaires, but it was for Irish freedom.'[12] J.M. Regan interprets de Valera's statement to the Dáil as follows: 'the assertion that Sinn Féin was not doctrinaire was also an admission that the republic of Easter week 1916, reiterated in the 1919 Declaration of Independence, had been a rhetorical and aspirational device, not descriptive fact'.[13] Both Lee and Regan show that in the summer of 1921, de Valera, in statesman-like fashion, while re-evaluating his own position with regard to the nature of the oath and the attainability of a republic, was also trying to open the minds of doctrinaire republicans to do likewise. As Lee concludes, to achieve an accommodation with Britain, 'he realised the inevitability of compromise'.[14]

ÉAMON DE VALERA MEETS LLOYD GEORGE

De Valera met with Lloyd George four times: on 14, 15, 18 and 21 July 1921. All four discussions took place at No. 10 Downing Street. Hopkinson states that these early efforts at exchanging views and teasing out issues 'amounted to elaborate verbal sparring sessions – not surprising given the character of the two participants'.[15] Referring to the knowledge that de Valera gained of Lloyd George's position, P.S. O'Hegarty asks acidly, 'is anyone so foolish as to believe that when Mr de Valera was closeted with Lloyd George for a week that they were discussing independence', and asserts that it is likely that 'Mr de Valera at the interviews, ascertained exactly how far England was prepared to go'.[16] Lee also holds this view and states that from the British point of view, Lloyd George succeeded in establishing, to his own satisfaction, 'during a protracted bout of sparring with de Valera following the Truce, that the achievement of a republic through negotiation was impossible'.[17] However, at this stage de Valera had merely engaged in teasing out the British position and testing their resolve. He did not reveal his own position at any stage to the British Prime Minister, nor, indeed, to the Irish cabinet or Dáil Éireann.

While the president strove to set out the Irish negotiating position, the Truce was being well received throughout Cork county. The people of Cork city continued 'to signify their appreciation of the Truce'. In Kanturk, the Truce 'was received with feelings of unalloyed satisfaction and profound relief', and in Charleville the announcement of the Truce 'was received with feelings of general satisfaction', and everybody 'fervently hoped' that the Truce 'was a prelude of happier days to come'.[18]

The verbal jousting between the British and Irish leaders turned into a prolonged correspondence. Hopkinson notes: 'between 21 July and 30 September fifteen telegrams and letters were exchanged which centred on the need to find some form of words on the identity of the Dáil government which would enable a full conference to begin'.[19] It can be assumed that both de Valera and Lloyd George became fully apprised of each other's position. However, despite his knowledge of the British position and his political stature, de Valera was making little progress in bringing home to the diehard doctrinaire republicans that the *realpolitik* of 1921 meant that a republic involving full internal and external self-determination appeared to be unattainable in the short term through negotiation.

The acrimonious tone of the correspondence and the continuous restating of the leaders' respective positions resulted in little progress. Lloyd George eventually wrote to de Valera on 7 September to ask whether Sinn Féin would agree to a conference whose purpose was 'to ascertain how the association of Ireland with the community of nations known as the British Empire can best be reconciled with Irish national aspirations'.[20] The crucial word in the letter is 'how', because this implies compromise. Lee supports this interpretation when he says that 'so scholastic a scrutineer of texts as de Valera can hardly have overlooked the significance of "how" rather than "whether" in this formula, which already contained the seeds of compromise'.[21] Lee also asserts that when de Valera accepted the invitation to a conference on the basis of the letter, he 'realised that the Republic was unattainable in the short term … Compromise was inevitable. The crude realities of power politics made some form of association with the British Empire unavoidable.'[22]

A grave situation arose on Thursday 15 September when Lloyd George cancelled the proposed conference at Inverness after the Sinn Féin envoys delivered a letter reiterating the claim that the Irish delegation would negotiate 'as the representatives of an independent or sovereign state'.[23] In his reply Lloyd George stated: 'I informed your emissaries who came to me here on Tuesday the 13th that the reiteration of your claim to negotiate with His Majesty's government as the representatives of an independent and sovereign state would make conference between us impossible'.[24] The *Cork Examiner* of 17 September reported on the consternation in Dublin at the news that the conference would not take place as expected. It stated: 'The people are absolutely stunned by the announcement that the Inverness conference on which so much hope had been built was cancelled.'

However, the crisis did not affect the atmosphere at an aeridheacht, an open-air festival, held in Charleville on 18 September. At the aeridheacht, 'the attendance reached huge dimensions' and the fixture was 'recorded as one of the most enjoyable and most successful held in the province for many years'.[25] Seán Moylan TD – column commander of Cork No. 2 brigade – addressed the meeting. He did not allude to the Inverness crisis or the negotiating stance adopted by Éamon de Valera, but concentrated on telling the assembly that the 'republican movement had its roots sprung deep from the Gaelic League', and that the 'Charleville Gaelic League should have a proper revolutionary outlook'. He dampened peace expectations by saying that he was not 'confident about the war being over'. He added: 'I am not looking for war; we all want peace if it is possible to get it; but we mean to have our freedom.'[26] He did not elaborate on what he meant by 'freedom' or what a 'proper revolutionary outlook' entailed. Neither did he make any attempt to prepare the attendance at the aeridheacht for the probability that de Valera could not enter into negotiations with the British government representing the people as president of an Irish republic. The tone of his language indicated that compromise was not on his agenda, and he certainly did not intimate to the assembly that 'freedom' might mean something less than a full-blown republic.

When de Valera finally did accept an invitation to a conference to be held in London on 11 October, he had dropped the claim that the Irish delegates would only negotiate as representatives of a sovereign Irish republic. Younger says that he merely asserted that he and Lloyd George had stated their 'respective positions' and agreed that a 'conference, not correspondence, is the most practical and hopeful way of achieving an understanding'.[27] De Valera's publicly declared position was still for internal and external self determination. The challenge for him was how to negotiate a treaty incorporating external self-determination for Ireland within the context of the contemporary British Empire. External self-determination implied that the Irish people had the right to choose the sovereignty under which they lived. If the British conceded this right it opened the way for possible rejection of the crown by de Valera, the Dáil and the Irish people.

DE VALERA'S NEGOTIATING STRATEGY

De Valera's search for a formula incorporating a compromise tailored to the Irish position was complicated by the Irish military situation. Militarily, 'he knew that Sinn Féin could not force Britain to recognise a completely independent Republic and that this demand also impeded Irish unification'.[28] At the Sinn Féin ard fheis in October 1921 de Valera outlined the problem he faced with regard to negotiation: 'The problem is to devise a scheme that will not detract from Irish freedom ... What may happen I am not able to judge, you should realise the difficulties that are in the way and the fact that the best people might differ on such a scheme.'[29]

Differences were becoming apparent at local levels, especially in North Cork. Another aeridheacht was held in Mallow on Sunday 25 September. The meeting was addressed by the lord mayor of Cork, Donal O'Callaghan TD, and by Seán Moylan TD. The lord mayor said that 'there was no change whatever in the present situation regarding Ireland's freedom ... the whole Irish nation desired peace, provided that peace meant their independence', and that 'they would fight as long as it was sought to enslave them'. Seán Moylan supported the sentiment expressed in the lord mayor's speech, and elaborated upon it: 'no Irishman wanted the perpetuation of English domination for Ireland'. He further stated that 'the fabric of nationality had been built up and as long as grass grew or water ran Ireland would not be turned down'.[30] Neither speaker referred to the impending negotiations, nor to the possibility that compromise might be necessary to achieve freedom and an end to English domination of Ireland by peaceful means.

To achieve that compromise, de Valera had been working upon what is widely regarded as a 'constitutionally brilliant concept of external association'.[31] J.M. Regan states that: 'Crushed by the immense pressures of Irish revolutionary republicanism and British imperialism de Valera produced a brilliant, if unpolished, constitutional diamond in his scheme for external association.'[32] Younger says: 'De Valera was about a quarter of a century ahead of his time', and he outlines how 'India, a republic associated with the Commonwealth, enjoys today exactly the status ... [that de Valera] envisaged for Ireland at that time'.[33] In correspondence with Lloyd George in mid-August, de Valera revealed this alternative to dominion status. He outlined the concept as follows:

A certain treaty of free association with the British Commonwealth group, as with a partial league of nations, we would
have been ready to recommend, and as a government to
negotiate and take responsibility for, had we an assurance that
the entry of the nation as a whole into such an association
would secure for it the allegiance of the present dissenting
minority, to meet whose sentiment alone this step could be
contemplated.[34]

However, according to Younger, Lloyd George interpreted external
association as meaning Ireland's secession from its allegiance to
the crown, and stated in his reply some days later that this was a
point 'upon which no British government can compromise'.[35]

Regardless of Lloyd George's uncompromising response, de
Valera set external association as his goal and, to achieve this, he
had a negotiating strategy developed that would be 'held together
by a compromise that would radiate from him'.[36] If negotiations
were finally concluded incorporating external association and if all
parties agreed a draft treaty, that treaty would be presented to the
cabinet and then to the Dáil. Because of his pre-eminent position
de Valera 'would carry the cabinet, the cabinet would carry the
Dáil and, crucially, the Dáil would carry the army in what was
to be a hierarchy of responsibility'.[37] Regan says: 'The evidence
suggests that in the certainty that the British would not concede
external association, de Valera envisaged a contingency whereby
the British would have to be pushed to the brink of war' to force
them to concede.[38] De Valera was well aware that, according to
the Truce, seventy-two hours' notice of a resumption of hostilities
had to be given by either side. This provision allowed ample time
for intervention. Bill Kissane suggests de Valera calculated that
'the British government would not resort to war for the difference
between Dominion status and his formula for a republic externally
associated with the Empire and he was willing to risk a resumption
of war to verify that assumption'.[39] However, if this transpired,

at the eleventh hour de Valera 'would be free to intervene and to strike the best possible compromise'.[40] In another scenario, if, as instructed, the Irish negotiators engineered the collapse of negotiations over the issue of the North, and there was a threat of war, de Valera would again intervene. If a treaty was brought to cabinet not incorporating external association, de Valera's hope was that both the cabinet and the Dáil would reject it. This has been argued by two writers: Hopkinson says: 'de Valera had hoped of there being a majority in the cabinet, and then in the Dáil, to oppose the Treaty',[41] whilst Sheila Lawlor supports Hopkinson's reading of the situation by saying that in the Treaty debate, de Valera did not 'take a decision himself, but probably hoped that the cabinet and the Dáil would share his feelings: the cabinet rejecting the document and the Dáil following suit'.[42] In the event of cabinet rejection, and particularly in the event of a breakdown over the North, de Valera's strategy was, as Regan says, to intervene so as to 'cause the British the most discomfiture before the international community and imbue Sinn Féin with the greatest moral authority' by causing the break in negotiations on the issue of partition. He would then play 'the trump nationalist card that they were not rejecting the crown but defending the integrity of their national territory'.[43] Then, through personal negotiation, de Valera would achieve the best possible terms for a settlement – specifically, external association. In these circumstances and under international scrutiny, it would be difficult for Lloyd George to initiate war.

NEGOTIATIONS BEGIN

On 9 September the representatives to travel to the conference in London were chosen by the Dáil ministry, subject to approval by the Dáil. However, Hopkinson states that the 'negotiators were de Valera's choice of delegates' and he criticises de Valera's choice, saying, 'the Irish negotiators were appointed neither for their personal suitability nor for their potential effectiveness as a team ... the personal and institutional tensions existing before the Truce were compounded by de Valera's choice of delegates'.[44] He also alleges that the delegates were appointed to appease the various elements within the Sinn Féin coalition, saying that 'neither Barton nor Duffy were leading figures within Sinn Féin', and that Duffy and Eamonn Duggan were 'legal padding'.[45] Moreover, 'Robert Barton and George Gavan Duffy, together with Erskine Childers as secretary, were meant to represent de Valera's interests' at the negotiations.[46] Both Barton and Duffy were to play crucial parts – Barton and Duffy in the London negotiations, and Barton in the cabinet vote on the Treaty. Unfortunately for de Valera, their actions did not serve his best interests as he had expected.

Neeson outlines the credentials given to the delegates by de Valera as president of the Dáil. They were appointed 'Envoys Plenipotentiary of the Republic of Ireland to negotiate and conclude on behalf of Ireland, with the representatives of His Majesty George V, a treaty or treaties of settlement'.[47] However, despite this flattering title, the written instructions given to the delegates states in section 2: 'Before decisions are finally reached on a main question, that a dispatch notifying the intention to make these decisions will be sent to members of the cabinet in Dublin', while section 3 says, 'it is also understood that a complete text of the draft treaty about to be signed will be submitted to Dublin, and reply awaited'.[48] As Neeson explains, 'the credentials and the written instructions were apparently contradictory. On the one hand, the words 'conclude on behalf of Ireland' gave the impression that the delegates had full plenipotentiary powers; their instructions, on the other hand, made it clear that they had no such power.[49] Hopkinson supports the assertion that the credentials were contradictory: 'There was

… a crucial inconsistency between the pledge to refer back any settlement and the full plenipotentiary powers given to the delegates'.[50]

In substance, 'de Valera in effect paralysed the delegation from the outset in terms of its ability to make a collective decision on any proposal which fell short of external association'.[51] The delegates, unsurprisingly believed themselves to be full plenipotentiaries. However, from the delegates' point of view, as the negotiations progressed, de Valera's position 'became more and more confused' because 'he refused either to lead or to negotiate'.[52] However, if Regan has correctly interpreted de Valera's strategy to step in at the eleventh hour to save the negotiations, this was all part of his plan. De Valera knew that it was only by testing Britain's resolve to the limit that a deal could be obtained that might bring the doctrinaire republicans on board.

However, Younger concisely describes the ultimate outcome of de Valera's attempts to control the delegates:

> They were to have plenary powers. But having handed the ball to his team, de Valera tied a string to it. The plenipotentiaries were not to sign any agreement without first referring it to Dublin. But so vigorously was the game played between the Irish and English teams that the string was jerked out of the president's hands.[53]

De Valera's eleventh-hour negotiating strategy precluded him from leading the plenipotentiaries to London. Some authors suggest that de Valera did not lead the Irish delegation for a variety of other reasons. Frank O'Connor, in his biography of Michael Collins, *The Big Fellow*, says that Collins felt that de Valera did not lead the delegation because, 'de Valera wished him to make concessions which de Valera himself, as president of the Irish republic, could not in all decency make'.[54] Younger suggests:

[De Valera's] decision not to lead the delegation to parley
with Lloyd George's team was implemented only by reason
of his own casting vote in the cabinet. He considered that
by remaining in Ireland, remote from the fray, he could
more effectively act as a brake if the delegates seemed to be
carried away in the heat of the argument, and, further, that
his presence was needed to restrain the impatience and the
bellicosity of Brugha and, to a lesser extent, Stack.[55]

Seán McEoin stated: 'Mr de Valera knew that he personally
could not get any more than what he had already been offered by
Lloyd George in London'.[56] However, in his assessment of the
negotiation team, Younger says that while it needed men of the
stature of Griffith and Collins, above all, it needed de Valera.[57]
Hopkinson supports this view when he quotes Cosgrave saying
that if de Valera was not in the delegation, 'it was equivalent to
leaving your best player in reserve'.[58] Lee suggests that de Valera
did not go to London because 'he apparently hoped that if he
were not involved in the negotiations himself, he could wean the
doctrinaires into accepting external association as an honourable
solution'.[59] When Lawlor refers to de Valera not going to London, she argues that 'perhaps his interviews and his correspondence with Lloyd George had convinced him that he could not
bring back what he wanted and that Collins would drive the
hardest bargain with Lloyd George'.[60] However, it seems likely
that de Valera's best guess was that negotiations would break
down, the gap between external association and allegiance to the
British monarch could not be bridged, and his most effective
position would be at home, not on the negotiating team. War
would be declared by the British, and he, at the eleventh hour,
would enter the negotiations and obtain the best terms possible
for Ireland. Referring to the necessity to keep the doctrinaire
republicans onside, Regan states: 'de Valera's imprimatur was to
be a prerequisite for the compromise now in view, having any

chance of holding the militarist-republicans within the terms of the settlement'.[61] However, for de Valera's strategy, as outlined by Regan, to work, it was crucial that the talks would work out as anticipated by him.

When Éamon de Valera accepted Lloyd George's reissued invitation to talks in London on 11 October on behalf of the Dáil, the *Cork Examiner* noted that the news 'was received in Cork with the utmost satisfaction', and that 'approval of the attitude of the Dáil was expressed on all sides'. The decision was considered 'a very important step towards the attainment of a settlement of national affairs'. De Valera's acceptance letter to Lloyd George stated that their 'respective positions have been stated and are understood'. What the people, and particularly the Volunteers, may not have understood is that de Valera's position needed to be tailored to meet that of Lloyd George.

The *Cork Examiner* of 18 October reported that 'a large Republican Army review was held at Milltown Cross, Newtown' near Charleville, and that 'upwards of 2,000 people witnessed the review'. The report says that the review was limited to drills and other military manoeuvres. However, it is significant that no speeches were made at the review to enlighten the Volunteers or the onlookers as to the progress of the London negotiations and the implications a settlement could have for the people of North Cork, and especially for the officers and men of Cork No. 4 brigade.[62]

DIFFICULTIES BETWEEN THE PLENIPOTENTIARIES AND THE CABINET

Negotiations continued from October until December. The final agreed draft of the Treaty was 'delivered to Sinn Féin on the evening of December 1', and, at Griffith's request, the British agreed 'to defer formal presentation until December 6'.[63] In accordance with the plenipotentiary's credentials, Griffith wrote to de Valera saying that 'it was essential to discuss the British proposals and he asked the president to call a cabinet meeting for the morning of Saturday, December 3.'[64]

Members of the Irish cabinet and delegation assembled at 11 a.m. on Saturday 3 December. This was 'the first time since the beginning of the negotiations that all delegates and the Dáil cabinet had met together'.[65] However, there was no unity in the cabinet on the merits of the draft treaty. Griffith stated 'his willingness to accept recognition of the crown, while de Valera stressed his opposition to any form of allegiance'.[66] Brugha, true to form, attacked 'the way that the negotiations had been conducted in sub-conferences, commenting "that the British had picked the weakest men in the delegation for that purpose!"'[67] The meeting was an unstructured, torrid affair. Afterwards, Collins complained to Tom Cullen – a member of his old 'Squad' – that 'he didn't know where he stood'.[68] Hopkinson notes that no agreed document came out of the meeting to set against the British draft treaty, and 'crucially there was no discussion on what the delegation's tactics should be' if Lloyd George continued to force the pace and 'refuse them time to consult their Dublin colleagues before signing the treaty'.[69] But Curran's view differs substantially from Hopkinson's. He believes that 'as the delegates made ready to return to London, the cabinet confirmed its main decisions'.[70] These decisions included the following:

- The delegates were to carry out their original instructions with the same powers.
- Griffith was to inform Lloyd George that the document could not be signed, to state that it was now a matter for the Dáil to decide and to try to place the blame for a break on Ulster.
- The president would not join the delegation in London at this stage.[71]

In substance, Younger agrees with Curran when he states that Griffith's instructions:

> … in so far as can be ascertained from the exiguous notes taken by the acting secretary, Colm O'Murchadha, were to refuse the suggested oath unless it was amended, to refuse to sign the Agreement and to inform the British that it was a matter for the Dáil. The break was to come on the Ulster issue.[72]

Curran says: 'Childers sought clarification. Did the demand for alteration of the oath mean rejection of Dominion status? De Valera said it did, which meant that external association must be presented again.'[73] But the reintroduction of external association at this stage was probably futile:

> De Valera must have known as well as Griffith that to offer to the British the formula he put forward now, what was to become known as Document No. 2, was like offering a three-legged donkey instead of the normal quadruped already promised in sale. Griffith's attitude was that the three-legged animal had already been offered.[74]

Curran summarises: 'In the end the cabinet gave the delegates neither an alternative proposal on Ulster nor even explicit instructions to turn down the British proposal; this would make it very hard to stage a break on the issue of partition, however desirable that might be.'[75] Regan says with some insight: 'It must have occurred to the plenipotentiaries, as they prepared to return to London on the evening of 3 December, that they were being sent to collapse the talks, not to conclude them.'[76]

The last point in Curran's summary of the cabinet decisions – 'The president would not join the delegation in London at this stage' – seems to imply that de Valera did originally intend to join the delegation and intervene at a late stage in the negotiations.

Because this session was the crucial stage, Regan legitimately asks: 'Why, if he intended to intervene, did de Valera chose not to lay his strategy before the cabinet and the plenipotentiaries?'[77] It can be easily understood that: 'The delegation returned to London for the final bout of negotiations confused and exhausted with the numbing instructions to succeed or commit the country to war. De Valera did not take the opportunity to outline any contingency strategy if the talks failed, other than war.'[78] Inexplicably, no instructions were given to contact de Valera in an emergency. Regan asserts that this was 'in the circumstances, not so much an oversight as a strategy'.[79]

THE LAST ROUND IN LONDON

Having returned to London, 'Griffith and his colleagues bravely began the wearisome argument again. They knew their arguments would be rejected.'[80] Regan summarises: 'external association remained outside the British offer as it emerged by the beginning of December'; this offer was 'full Dominion rights with the same status in law and in practice as Canada'.[81] Younger recounts a gaffe made by George Gavin Duffy during negotiations: 'Lloyd George expressed amazement at the delegation's difficulty in accepting clauses 1, 2, 3, of the proposals. "Our difficulty," answered Duffy, "is to come into the Empire, looking on all that has happened in the past." "In that case, it's war," snapped Lloyd George.'" According to Younger, 'Duffy's spontaneous words crushed the opportunity Griffith had been angling for ... to force the break on Ulster.'[82] Regan agrees with Younger: 'Owing to Gavan Duffy's slip the conference had collapsed on the condition of inclusion in the Empire and on recognition of the crown and not on Ulster.'[83] Duffy, representing de Valera, had made a crucial mistake.

A written pledge from Griffith to Lloyd George to strengthen his position at the Conservative meeting in Liverpool on 17

November added to the problems of the Irish negotiators. The pledge 'provided that Northern Ireland could exclude itself from an all-Ireland parliament, but if it did, a commission would adjust the Irish boundary to make it conform as closely as possible to the wishes of the population'.[84] Later, during negotiations, Lloyd George declared that 'the Irish were trying to stage a break on Ulster because their cabinet had refused membership of the Empire'.[85] In a last throw of the dice, says Curran, Griffith 'appealed to the prime minister to ask Craig if Ulster would accept unity on condition Sinn Féin accepted crown and Empire'.[86] Lloyd George refused, dramatically producing Griffith's written pledge, and Griffith was beaten. 'The prime minister destroyed Griffith's chance to break on Ulster and ensured his acceptance of the Treaty.'[87] Griffith's injudicious pledge further damaged the already weakened Irish position created by Duffy's mistake.

Griffith's agreement to sign the Treaty forced the other delegates to a decision. Collins was acutely aware of the weakened military position of the IRA and the ordeal suffered by the people. Moreover, he 'was convinced that Ireland could not get substantially better terms and that the alternative to settlement was war and defeat'. He agonised over his decision, and, as the Irish delegates' taxi returned from negotiations, 'announced he intended to sign the Treaty'.[88] A heated debate about the Treaty ensued among the delegates. The result was that Duggan agreed to sign and made an impassioned and successful appeal to Barton to do likewise. The isolated Duffy 'caved in shortly afterward and a united, if miserable, delegation was prepared to accept the Treaty'.[89] Duffy's negotiating blunder and his decision, with Barton, to sign, meant that de Valera's plans had gone badly awry. The die was now cast. Regan says de Valera's strategy, as well as his authority, was beginning to crumble in London.[90] Consequently, the fate of the Treaty lay in the hands of the Irish cabinet and Dáil Éireann.

THE PLENIPOTENTIARIES RETURN WITH THE TREATY

De Valera had no prior knowledge of the signing of the Treaty. He 'received the Treaty with sour disappointment and was incensed by the failure of the plenipotentiaries to consult him before they signed'.[91] Hopkinson says that 'de Valera, on being shown the terms, was aghast and talked of being insulted by the failure to consult',[92] while Regan explains that 'what had gone wrong in London from de Valera's point of view was that the plenipotentiaries had not gone the distance, refused to gamble and failed to call the British hand'.[93] Younger asks: 'Was he perhaps piqued that he had had no opportunity to step in at the last minute as "an honest broker"?'[94] Here, he supports Regan's idea that de Valera had intended to enter negotiations at the eleventh hour as a final arbiter in order to gain 'the maximum concessions from the British' by exploiting to the full 'the very reason why the British had decided to parley in the first instance; their reluctance either to extend or to escalate the war in Ireland'.[95]

De Valera called a cabinet meeting for 7 December and issued the following press statement: 'In view of the nature of the proposed treaty with Great Britain, President de Valera has sent an urgent summons to the members of the cabinet in London to report at once so that a full cabinet decision may be taken.' Referring to the press statement, Coogan says, 'this was the first open step taken in the direction of Civil War. Ominous notes were being sounded'.[96] It was at this point 'that de Valera began the process whereby he determined publicly to separate himself from the signatories and the document itself'.[97]

Coogan quotes a further press statement issued by de Valera in which he states: 'The terms of this agreement are in violent conflict with the wishes of the majority of this nation as expressed freely in successive elections during the past three years.'[98] That may be the interpretation de Valera put on those elections, but while he may have been speaking to the militarist-republican constituency, it is hard to believe that he was unaware of the attitude of the ordinary people to the Treaty. The *Irish Times* of 9 December referring to the Treaty, affirmed that 'the whole Nationalist Press and, as we believe, the vast majority of southern Irishmen have accepted it with joy'.[99] Curran summarises the countrywide reaction to the Treaty:

> In Ireland the national press was jubilant over the settlement. Leading newspapers in southern Ireland hailed it as a great advance that would bring freedom and, it was hoped, unity. Catholic bishops supported the Treaty, not only because it held out the prospect of national freedom and unity, but also because it promised an end to the violence which seriously threatened morality and clerical authority. An impressive number of public and private bodies also expressed approval of the settlement.[100]

Younger supports this positive reception of the Treaty: 'News of the Treaty had brought to the majority of the people of Ireland immeasurable joy and relief … [it was] rash of de Valera to claim that the Treaty was in violent conflict with the wishes of the majority.'[101] The Treaty was very well received in the Charleville area. The *Cork Examiner* of 8 December reported that 'the successful termination of the Anglo-Irish Peace Conference was received with general rejoicing in Charleville and district', and that 'in all quarters there is evidence of the profound gratification at the triumph of the negotiations'. Indeed, the 'victory' was considered 'a glorious one for the patriotic and self-sacrificing members of the Dáil cabinet'.

Hopkinson suggests that some commentators 'have attributed de Valera's opposition to the Treaty to what P.S. O'Hegarty called wounded vanity, a resentment of the fact that he had lost control of events'. He quotes T. Ryle Dwyer writing that de Valera's attitude was 'influenced by his determination to show that he, not Collins, was the real leader', and Ronan Fanning arguing that de Valera 'opposed the Treaty not because it was a compromise but because it was not his compromise'.[102] Others support the suggestion that de Valera was piqued at the signing of the Treaty without his consent: 'A settlement reached by de Valera in London … would have made a difference for simply being de Valera's settlement.'[103]

De Valera would have been counting on Barton's vote in the cabinet, for or against the Treaty. However, he had miscalculated and 'slipped into the course from which he subsequently failed to extricate himself: he did not take a decision himself, but probably hoped that the cabinet and the Dáil would share his feelings: the cabinet rejecting the document and the Dáil following suit'.[104] In the cabinet, however, the decision was otherwise. On 8 December, five members of the cabinet declared themselves in favour of recommending the Treaty to the Dáil. The five were Griffith, Collins, Barton, Cosgrave and O'Higgins – though the latter had no vote.[105] Barton courageously voted for the Treaty he had signed in London. His vote, with that of Cosgrave, Collins and Griffith, meant that a cabinet majority favoured the Treaty. De Valera now had to depend on a Dáil majority to reject it.

The Dáil met on 14 December, and shortly afterwards went into private session until 17 December. The contradictory terms of reference issued to the plenipotentiaries by de Valera immediately became an issue. Hopkinson says that 'at the start of the Dáil Treaty debates de Valera admitted that the plenipotentiaries had not exceeded their powers by signing the Treaty without consulting Dublin first'.[106] In contrast, Lawlor says that de Valera referred to 'the failure of the delegates to obey their instructions and submit the final draft of the document to Dublin before signing'.[107] Younger reports de Valera as saying that 'his quarrel with the plenipotentiaries was that they had signed the Treaty without submitting the final text to Dublin'.[108] Adding to the confusion, Collins argued that they had signed the Treaty 'on the understanding that each signatory would recommend the instrument to the Dáil'.[109] These conflicting arguments are due to the ambiguity of the original instructions to the plenipotentiaries. Clarity regarding the terms of reference issued by de Valera and specific instructions to contact him in an emergency would have avoided the acrimony evident in the opening Dáil exchanges.

Hopkinson argues that 'de Valera's opposition to the Treaty was more complex than that of most anti-Treatyites'. He says that 'de Valera adopted a detached position from that of the republican diehards', and that 'de Valera's central preoccupation had been unity'.[110] De Valera himself stated:

> My task was to try and get by negotiations something which would satisfy Britain, something which would satisfy what I may call the left wing of the cabinet and something which would satisfy the right wing. The left wing of the cabinet was for an isolated Republic for the most part, but I pulled them over a bit … while I was pulling along that wing, the other wing got away from me.[111]

Lee notes that at this point de Valera was preoccupied with keeping Sinn Féin unified and even as early as October 1921, he had realised that to do this compromise would be inevitable.[112] De Valera also wanted to re-assert his leadership, and he 'attempted to win back the political initiative from Collins and Griffith by introducing his hastily drafted Document No. 2 on the second day of the private session'.[113] Hopkinson says: 'In a vain attempt to recover control, de Valera submitted his Document No. 2 which amounted to a rewriting of the proposals he had submitted during the London negotiations.'[114] But as Younger notes: 'Those who supported the Treaty could not see that de Valera's document was any more than a quibble. It was a compromise, just as the

Treaty was a compromise. Those who opposed the Treaty could not see that de Valera's proposal was very different [from the Treaty].'[115] Moreover, despite the merits of the concept, 'external association [was not] easily understood and could not be communicated effectively to the public. It still contained the idea that Ireland would be part of the Commonwealth with recognition that the British crown headed that Commonwealth.'[116]

Griffith insisted that de Valera's proposal be discussed in public session because, as Coogan explains: 'The document showed that de Valera was not standing as the living symbol of the Republic, but as someone who favoured a compromise similar to that on offer.'[117] As a result, 'de Valera's Document No. 2 and his external association formula did not have the symbolic appeal of either the Republic or Dominion status and it got little support'.[118] In fact, it seems that: 'The introduction of Document No. 2 hardened the Treatyites' resolve. It exposed how close de Valera was prepared to come to the Treaty in seeking a settlement – and the incomprehension of external association and its dismissal as a mere quibble accentuated the effect.'[119] From the republicans' standpoint, external association as a compromise was stillborn, because any semblance of the presence of the crown in Irish affairs was anathema to them. Regan concludes: 'Tactically, its introduction so early in the debate was a gross miscalculation. Neither the doctrinaire republicans, pro-Treaty deputies, nor those occupying the no-man's land of the undecided, were prepared to attempt to find any common ground within its provisions, and Document No. 2 was ignominiously withdrawn by its author.'[120]

This was a major political setback for de Valera and he found himself isolated. Lawlor succinctly sums up his position: 'de Valera was now without a plan, without power, and in the eyes of many who had heard him propose Document No. 2, without his principles intact.'[121] His strategy for intervening at the eleventh hour in the event of Treaty rejection and threat of war was in tatters. Lee states that 'his real blunder was less conspiracy than miscalculation. He staked everything on preserving unity through his external association scheme. De Valera had no contingency plans.'[122] On 7 January the Treaty was approved by sixty-four votes to fifty-seven and de Valera subsequently resigned as president. He was not re-elected. Collins proposed Griffith as the new president of the Dáil, whereupon de Valera left the chamber with a number of his supporters. Griffith was duly elected. De Valera's main supporters had always been hard-line, doctrinaire republicans, and because he was outmanoeuvred in the Dáil, he was now in their camp. At this stage, irreconcilable differences made civil war a distinct probability.

DE VALERA CHANGES COURSE

It is difficult to understand the course de Valera took next in view of some of his previously stated positions on democracy. When the cabinet voted in favour of the Treaty, de Valera wrote to the press revealing the split in the cabinet. He stated, reassuringly, that 'there is a definite constitutional way of resolving our political differences', and added: 'Let the conduct of the cabinet in this matter be an example to the whole nation.'[123] Here, he seemed to be advocating democratic decisions based on majority rule. While de Valera was now solidly in the anti-Treatyite camp, Younger notes that it 'appeared he was prepared to battle exclusively in the political arena, when, on March 15, the formation of Cumann na Poblachta, or the League of the Republic, was announced over his signature as President.'[124] Commenting on his status, Lee says: 'in moral and political stature he stood head and shoulders above everyone on the anti-Treaty side',[125] while Lawlor asserts that 'de Valera's leaving the Dáil has acquired in retrospect some symbolic value as representing his rejection of constitutional methods'.[126] Kissane expresses the view that 'his loss of authority may well be the explanation for his occasionally reckless behaviour over the following months'.[127]

De Valera was in the republican camp with divisional commanders such as Liam Lynch, whose creed was outlined by O'Donoghue: 'we have declared for a Republic and will not live under any other law!'[128] Lee suggests that in trying to achieve some control and authority over uncompromising, doctrinaire republicans such as Lynch, 'de Valera made speeches which seemed to be inciting to [*sic*] civil war, though he himself maintained that he was simply warning against the danger in his own inimitable way'.[129] Younger recounts that 'in Dungarvan, County Waterford, de Valera made the first of a series of inflammatory speeches. It is impossible to believe, despite de Valera's denial of any intention to incitement, that these words were meant to convey other than what they plainly said.'[130] Notable remarks from the speeches included:

- Dungarvan, 16th March: It was only by civil war after this that they could get their independence.
- Tipperary, St Patrick's Day: If the Treaty were not rejected, perhaps it was over the bodies of the young men he saw around him that day that the fight for Irish freedom may be fought.
- Thurles: If they accepted the Treaty, and if the Volunteers of the future tried to complete the work the Volunteers of the last four years had been attempting, they … would have to wade through Irish blood, through the blood of the soldiers of the Irish government, and through, perhaps, the blood of some of the members of the government in order to get Irish freedom.
- Killarney: These men in order to achieve freedom will have … to march over the dead bodies of their own brothers.[131]

Coogan describes these statements as 'inflammatory speech-making' which, he says, 'became an ineradicable blot' on the reputation of de Valera.[132] Referring to these speeches, Curran says:

> The historian's verdict can only be that de Valera's remarks, whatever their intent, were irresponsible and dangerous. Certainly, excitable young men with guns in their hands did not need the kind of warning de Valera gave. For a leader of his stature to utter prophecies of bloody domestic conflict only increased its likelihood.[133]

In his introduction to *The Victory of Sinn Féin* by P.S. O'Hegarty, Tom Garvin raises a disturbing issue. Referring to de Valera, he says, 'my suspicion is that his own actions led him to suffer a nervous breakdown in 1922 and he would in the eyes of a later generation be regarded as seriously ill during the period and not fully responsible for his actions'.[134] Kissane supports this assertion: 'The year 1922 is said to have induced a nervous breakdown in de Valera.'[135] However, neither author adduces any proof for their assertion as to de Valera's mental state. Hopkinson reminds us that 'time after time in the Dáil de Valera had to be reminded of how his speeches in the spring of 1922 contradicted his affirmation during the Treaty debates that a constitutional way should be found to resolve their differences'.[136] De Valera may have been issuing warnings about the dangers of civil war, but 'he may also have been trying to force Griffith and Collins to compromise'.[137] At best through his actions, de Valera lost personal credibility and placed himself in a very embarrassing position.[138] At worst, he was guilty of incitement to violence against the Provisional Government.

By March, the establishment of the Irish Free State was moving apace and the Treaty was ratified in both Houses of Parliament by the end of the month. Consequently, Hopkinson says that in the spring of 1922, de Valera 'was able to exercise little personal authority over events' and that he 'had become an increasingly isolated figure striving behind the scenes to win back his political influence'.[139] Lyons recounts how, at the spring Sinn Féin ard fheis, 'Griffith and de Valera had been able to meet and agree that no election would be held for three months'.[140] The election was finally fixed for 16 June. Regan argues that 'the logic of the situation as it pertained in Southern Ireland in spring 1922 was that no general election could be held without the cooperation of the anti-Treaty IRA'.[141] So Collins 'had a personal meeting with de Valera on 20 May at which their seven-point electoral pact was concluded'.[142] This rather complicated pact essentially laid out the provisions of who could stand and the make-up of the elected executive. Regan summarises the advantages of this electoral pact for both camps:

> The agreement suited de Valera in that it afforded him an opportunity to regroup and campaign and it postponed a looming and potentially devastating electoral defeat. The agreement was crucial for the Provisional Government in that it gave them breathing space to produce a constitution that if sufficiently republican in tone could draw the teeth of militant republicanism and avoid civil war. Deferral of the vote also afforded time to publicise the benefits of the Treaty, not least of which was the very public departure of British troops, and above all it gave them a chance to rebuild the machinery of state, including the new Civic Guard and the new Free State Army.[143]

Collins claimed that 'the pact was the only way of ensuring that the election would be held at all, given the anxiety of the anti-Treaty forces to prevent a popular verdict'.[144] Regan believes that 'this was the logic, which underpinned Collins' controversial decision to enter into a pact with de Valera in May'.[145] He outlines the nature of the pact as follows: 'the Collins–de Valera pact, ratified by the reconvened extraordinary ard fheis on 22 May, sought to replicate the second Dáil by offering the electorate a panel of Sinn Féin candidates in identical proportion to existing Treatyite and anti-Treatyite representation'.[146] Lee argues that: 'From de Valera's point of view, the pact had the attraction of continuing the political process [and] arresting the apparent inevitable slide towards war'. Furthermore, de Valera 'could hope to retrieve something of his former authority only if politics remained the medium of exchange.'[147] Curran notes that 'Griffith accepted the pact with the greatest reluctance. Since the April peace conference, he felt that nothing good could come from negotiating with de Valera, whom he regarded as dishonest as well as wrong.'[148]

Disturbingly, de Valera's somewhat ambivalent attitude towards democracy at this time can be seen in his support for diehard republican, Rory O'Connor, who, with the Dublin No. 1 brigade, had occupied the Four Courts in April, as a sign of republican opposition to the Treaty. De Valera described O'Connor and his fellow occupiers of the as 'the best and bravest of our nation'.[149] Lawlor also quotes de Valera saying, 'in Rory O'Connor and his men lives the unbought indomitable soul of Ireland',[150] and that through the actions of O'Connor and his followers in the Four Courts, 'the Republic was fighting for its life'.[151] However, Rory O'Connor did not see de Valera in the same light. In March, O'Connor displayed a measure of contempt for de Valera and his Document No. 2, describing it disparagingly as 'something which he had not read'.[152] Furthermore, de Valera's place on the political periphery from the republicans' point of view at that time can be deduced from O'Connor's admission that the 'Four Courts had been taken without consulting or even informing de Valera'.[153]

Kissane states that 'once the results of the June election became known the issue of democratic authority could not be repressed any longer'.[154] The pro-Treaty candidates won fifty-eight seats, while the anti-Treaty candidates won only thirty-six. The thirty-four remaining seats went to Labour, independents, Trinity College, and the Farmers party. Curran summarises the election result: 'Republicans in 1922 had no doubt about their defeat at the polls. De Valera conceded defeat before the final returns were counted, blaming it on Britain's threat of war.'[155]

In 1921, during his meetings with Lloyd George, Éamon de Valera was at the zenith of his political power in Ireland. Hopkinson summarises de Valera's position after the Treaty accurately when he says, 'the period between the Treaty and the end of the Civil War represented Éamon de Valera's political nadir'.[156] With the outbreak of war, republican and pro-Treaty militarists took control, and de Valera did not fill an effective political role in Ireland again until the late spring of 1923, when the Civil War was dragging inexorably to a conclusion. Many authors believe that the Civil War may not have happened if de Valera had supported the Treaty. It could equally be argued that if his negotiating strategy – as outlined above – had worked out, many who had reluctantly supported the republican side could have been weaned away from the extreme republican position, and that the Civil War – if it had happened at all – would have been on a much smaller scale. At any rate, his political isolation meant that he played a marginalised role during the course of the Civil War, and indeed, it could be argued that the loss of his political influence may have prolonged it.

REPUBLICAN CHALLENGE AND COLLAPSE IN BLESSINGTON

While the political wrangling was going on, events on the ground were reflecting the polarisation of the pro- and anti-Treaty sides. Throughout the spring and early summer of 1922, republicans both disregarded and challenged the authority of the Provisional Government. As the British forces withdrew under the Treaty agreement, a scramble for possession of their barracks ensued. Republicans were the main beneficiaries, especially in the south, and their military status was enhanced. On 26 March they held an army convention in defiance of a Provisional Government ban. Control of military resources was wrested from the Provisional Government when the convention 'reaffirmed the republican status of the army and agreed that the army should be brought back under the complete control of its executive'.[157] The most symbolic challenge to the Provisional Government was of course the occupation of the Four Courts. With this action, the authority of the Provisional Government was being publicly challenged: the building occupied by the republicans housed the chief law offices of the country, and, understandably, the 'occupation hugely alarmed British government circles'.[158]

In other areas of the country trouble was also brewing. A crisis arose in early March in Limerick as pro-Treaty and anti-Treaty forces sought to gain control of strategically important buildings being evacuated by British forces. Ernie O'Malley, commanding the republican 2nd Southern Division gave pro-Treaty forces in the Castle barracks twelve hours to vacate the premises. Michael Brennan, commander of the pro-Treaty forces, refused and a military showdown seemed inevitable. The republican forces, in terms of equipment and experienced men, held the advantage and Brennan demanded reinforcements and equipment, including a tank, from the Provisional Government. Arthur Griffith urged that all republican-held barracks be taken by force, but Collins and Mulcahy were dubious as to the merits of this proposal. Through the good offices of Liam Lynch and Mayor O'Mara of Limerick the stand-off was defused. The compromise hammered out between the parties involved Limerick Corporation holding the police barracks, outside troops returning to their own areas and small companies of republican forces holding two military barracks.

In early May a similar crisis arose in Kilkenny. Anti-Treaty forces took over Ormond Castle and the City Hall. Two hundred men from the Dublin Guard were dispatched by the Provisional Government to retake the buildings. They succeeded, after some fighting which led to a small number of casualties. A larger-scale military confrontation was once again avoided when an agreement was patched together that involved both parties sharing occupation of barracks in the city.

Meanwhile, republicans continued to arm themselves for conflict. In February, they raided Clonmel Royal Irish Constabulary (RIC) barracks, capturing a considerable quantity of arms, and the daring seizure of the British ship *Upnor* on the high seas in April netted them 200 lorry-loads of arms and ammunition. The government referred in the Dáil to '331 raids on post offices between 23 March and 19 April, and 319 attacks on the Great Southern and Western Railway by armed men between 1 March and 22 April'. Raids on the National Bank on 1 May, 'ordered by the army executive', netted nearly £50,000 for republicans.[159] Lack of Provisional Government control countrywide was being exposed, and the law was being freely flouted by republicans.

Hopkinson asserts that the large pro-Treaty majority in the election of 16 June 1922 'had an important role in legitimising the Treaty and the status of the Provisional Government'.[160] With this mandate, the Provisional Government could now assert its authority. However, the assassination of Sir Henry Wilson on 22 June created a major dilemma for the Provisional Government. The British establishment was incensed and demanded that action be taken immediately to remove the Four Courts garrison. General Macready was even ordered to prepare plans to attack the building with British forces and artillery. While Collins and Richard Mulcahy, minister of defence, could not afford to seem to be bowing to pressure from Churchill and Lloyd George, the kidnapping by republicans of General J.J. O'Connell, deputy chief-of-staff of the National Army, gave the Provisional Government the excuse it needed. This provocation finally triggered the attack on the Four Courts in the early morning of 28 June, when reluctant Provisional Government forces fired the first shots of the Civil War. The garrison surrendered after three days' shelling – together with the detonation of two mines that blasted the invaluable archives to shreds – and the republican garrison of 140 men were taken to Mountjoy prison.

General Eoin O'Duffy, chief-of-staff of the pro-Treaty forces, 'announced that the "revolt" was all over',[161] but he was mistaken. The republicans quickly occupied the east side of O'Connell Street, but this proved 'as militarily pointless as the Four Courts occupation had been'.[162] Over a number of days, the pro-Treaty forces closed in on the republicans in the Hammam Hotel, and 'de Valera and others were smuggled across the river to Mount Street'.[163] The Dublin city fighting is remembered as much for its futility as for the refusal of the pugnacious, but peerlessly brave, Cathal Brugha to surrender. With the Hammam Hotel blazing behind him, Brugha emerged from the building revolver in hand. He was cut down by Lewis gunfire and mortally wounded. His death 'in the tradition of Pearse, was a sublime declaration of the faith he had in his own convictions',[164] and many believed he planned it to be a rallying call for the republicanism by which he lived.

Hopkinson states that 'not for the first time in Irish history the postscript to fighting in Dublin occurred in the Dublin and Wicklow hills'.[165] It is baffling that the republicans here adopted the same strategy that had failed in the Four Courts and central Dublin. Neeson says that 'in Blessington O'Maille [Ernie O'Malley] took charge and decided to defend the area and straddle the route to the south'.[166] By Tuesday 2 July, 'the triangle [of] Blessington, Brittas, Kilbride was occupied', mines were laid, Lewis guns guarded the approaches and a field hospital was set up in the town.[167] Inevitably, 'more than a thousand Provisional Government troops from six bases began an encircling movement' on Blessington.[168] When contact was made at Brittas and Kilbride, the anti-Treatyites retreated. The unexpected capture of republicans Gerry Boland and Andy McDonnell, Dublin brigade and battalion commandants, caused O'Malley to seriously revise his strategy. Their capture at Crosschapel on the road between Kilteel and Hempstown confirmed the encirclement of his troops in Blessington and he decided to evacuate Blessington as soon as possible to avoid capture of his 800-strong force.[169]

There seems to have been little coherent strategy in the republican planning, and this was exemplified by Seán Moylan's expedition with 230 men to Wexford. Hopkinson says that his 'expedition proved a sorry failure'. He quotes Pax Whelan, the O/C of the Waterford Brigade, saying, 'they stayed a day or two in New Ross and they commandeered everything they could lay their hands on'. Consequently, 'his men made themselves unpopular in the locality'. Moylan formed the opinion that he would be better employed 'concentrating on Thurles, Nenagh and perhaps Kilkenny', since 'the local volunteers seem to be practically non-existent, and the few men we've met have been very little assistance to us'.[170] Hopkinson concludes that 'the expedition was a prime example of the failure of republican troops to work effectively outside their own areas', and that 'any hope of a successful south-eastern strategy' had ended for the republicans when 'it was reported on 7 July that 'O'Malley's men had left in a charabanc and a car in the direction of Carlow'.[171]

The focus of the two forces now switched to the south-west, and the area that the anti-Treaty forces had chosen as their defensive line – the Waterford–Limerick axis. The republican forces greatly outnumbered the Free State forces in Limerick and they believed that it would be very difficult for the pro-Treaty forces to capture Waterford. The city is protected from the north and east by the River Suir and a successful attack would entail crossing the river in force. Also Waterford was protected by the strongly republican areas of South Tipperary to the north and Cork to the west. Carrick-on-Suir, Clonmel and Golden were also held by republicans and they, with other smaller republican strongholds, formed the republican defensive line linking Limerick with Waterford. The area south-west of the line, including counties Cork, Kerry, Tipperary and south Limerick became known colloquially as 'The Republic of Munster' and the battle for this so-called 'Republic' was about to begin.

2

The Attack on the
'Republic of Munster'

THE BATTLE FOR LIMERICK

On 21 July 1922 the cities of Limerick and Waterford fell to
the pro-Treaty forces, and the subsequent fourteen-day battle
in the Kilmallock–Bruree–Bruff triangle had a decisive impact
on the geographical context and military progression of the
Civil War to its end. General Michael Brennan, Commandant
of the 1st Western Division of the National army stated that,
even many years afterwards it was still not fully appreciated
that 'the whole Civil War really turned on Limerick'.[1] Brennan
argued that 'the Shannon was the barricade and whoever held
Limerick held the south and the west'. Eoin Neeson agrees
with Brennan's assessment, stating that 'with both Limerick
and Waterford in Government hands all hope of defending the
'Republic of Munster' disappeared'.[2] However, he also believes
that the implications of the fall of Limerick led the pro-Treaty
authorities to over-optimistically assume 'that the war was
nearly over', which turned out not to be the case. Neeson even
asserts that 'de Valera favoured ending hostilities at this time'.[3]
Statements to this effect were issued by pro-Treaty leaders,
and jubilation was loud – but premature. In summary, Michael
Hopkinson concludes that 'in retrospect, both republican and
pro-Treaty participants held that the struggle for control of the
city decided the war.'[4]

With the withdrawal of British troops, National Army headquarters must have been well aware of the strategic value of Limerick. Consequently, Commandant Brennan 'was directed to occupy Limerick with troops of the 1st Western Division and such support as the 4th South Division could provide.'[5] Liam Lynch, republican CIC, also saw the strategic importance of Limerick, and having consolidated his rear by capturing Skibbereen in County Cork, Listowel in County Kerry and Adare in County Limerick, he set up his headquarters in New barracks, Limerick city, while his troops also occupied the Strand, Castle and Ordnance barracks.[6] Brennan received support from Donnchadh O'Hannigan, commandant of the 4th Southern, and they occupied the customs house, the jail, the courthouse, William Street barracks and Cruise's Hotel.[7] At this point, the republicans were in a dominant position in the city. Republican numbers in the city at this point amounted to over 700 men, considerably outnumbering the 400 troops under the command of O'Hannigan and Brennan.[8] Lynch had the added advantage of having experienced commanders under him, such as War of Independence veterans Seán Moylan and Liam Deasy. Younger outlines the precarious position of the pro-Treaty troops, stating that 'they could muster no more than 200 rifles', and recounts – somewhat amusingly – the subterfuges engaged in by Brennan in an attempt to outfox Lynch. He relates Brennan's men 'held lengths of piping to simulate Lewis guns', and how fifty rifles were recycled to his reinforcements, marching in relays into Limerick, to give republicans the impression that there was no shortage of rifles.[9]

Whether the republicans tumbled to the ruse or not, on 2 July 1922 Seán Moylan sought Lewis gunners from Cork No. 1 brigade who were stationed in Fermoy, and wrote to Liam Deasy, O/C 1st Southern Division saying:

> I must get 100 riflemen and 10 machine-guns and crews sent from Cork and Kerry at once. The Staters are in force and

well equipped and I must hold the offensive. Cork 1 can send a bunch of right good men, so can Kerry and let us have them. There is no use in fooling with this question any longer. Send on the men and let us get on with the work. What about sending us a few hundred grenades?[10]

Despite Moylan's aggressive stance, Liam Lynch stalled, and twice concluded what amounted to a truce with Brennan and O'Hannigan, on 4 July and 7 July 1922.[11] Neeson suggests that 'Lynch's purpose in these Limerick negotiations is far from clear', especially as he must have known that by 7 July the war was already ten days old and that the anti-Treaty forces in Dublin, Brittas and Blessington had been defeated.[12] Not only did these truce negotiations stir up republican dissent, but the also gave a clear advantage to the pro-Treaty forces, since 'on 11 July a consignment of arms, with 150 men and the same number of rifles, was sent to Limerick from Dublin via Galway and Clare'.[13]

The tentative truce broke down on 11 July, with recriminations on both sides. The republicans accused the pro-Treaty side of bad faith in not keeping to the terms of the agreements. However, it was the shooting in the back of a pro-Treaty soldier by republicans while erecting a barricade that provoked the pro-Treaty William Street post to open fire on the republican garrison in the Ordnance barracks.[14] Inevitably, the battle for Limerick had begun, and peace talks were replaced by the rattle of gunfire.

The early exchanges from entrenched positions were somewhat desultory. Eventually 'it settled down to raids, sorties and attacks on enemy positions with neither side gaining any decisive advantage'.[15] To their cost, the republican forces did not hammer home their clear initial advantage in numbers and weapons, and the Provisional Government forces were being reinforced daily. An alarmed Seán Hyde reported to Liam Deasy, republican O/C 1st Southern Division, on 11 July:

The situation here has got very serious during the last hour or so. FS troops have swarmed into the city like bees and occupied practically all the posts we had last week. Already casualties have been reported among our men who were erecting barricades. The enemy have a plentiful supply of armoured cars and steel-plated lorries. Firing occurs at intervals. Help, no matter how small, will be very welcome.[16]

The *Cork Examiner* of 14 July reported that republican assistance did materialise when 'reinforcements reached New barracks from Cork district', and in the same paper, the 'Irish Republican Army: official bulletin' announced that 'communications are working splendidly and our troops hold the initiative now'. However, the *Freeman's Journal* of 15 July states that pro-Treaty forces 'captured an important Irregular outpost' and that 'many Irregular snipers had been dislodged'.

Despite rushing 'Woolworths with bayonet and bomb' on 14 July at 11 a.m., and capturing 'the post without loss of men or material',[17] the attitude of the republican forces was largely defensive, a strategy that would ultimately prove not to be in their best interests. Neeson argues: 'no army ... acting purely on the defensive can hope to succeed, as the morale of the troops inevitably suffers', allowing the initiative to pass to the opposite side.[18] Lynch's decision to move republican HQ from Limerick city to Clonmel at this stage must have had a further unsettling effect on the republican defenders. There was growing unrest among republicans at the lack of aggression shown by their leadership, and this probably resulted in the subsequent loss of Limerick.[19] Neeson quotes Tom Barry saying, 'some of our leaders [military] were a joke in a revolutionary movement'. He also quotes an East Cork brigade officer saying, 'at no time did I see a plan of attack ... there was a complete absence of organised military efficiency'.[20]

The arrival of pro-Treaty artillery on 19 July and the incessant shelling of the Strand, Ordnance, New and Castle barracks, combined with the storming of the Strand barracks by Captain Con O'Halloran, signalled the end of republican dominance in Limerick.[21] Having fired their strongholds, the republicans evacuated the city, and 'in the early hours of Friday [21 July] a stream of cars and lorries whirled the republicans out of the city to the south'.[22]

There was clearly chagrin and incomprehension amongst the republican forces at this policy of truce and evacuation. Hopkinson quotes Mick Murphy of Cork No. 1 brigade commenting that 'we came back to Buttevant, but why we did not know', and he also quotes Jamie Managhan, another Cork No. 1 officer, recalling how: 'There was pandemonium … our men from Limerick were completely demoralised.'[23] Despite their disillusionment, the republicans dug in at the Bruff–Bruree–Kilmallock triangle, 'where they successfully delayed the pro-Treaty advance to the south for over two weeks'.[24]

THE KILMALLOCK STAND

The reasons why the republicans chose this area to make the next determined stand are clearly outlined by Neeson. Kilmallock was the first large town between Limerick city and the Cork border. It dominated the approaches to and from Cork, gave some cover to Kerry and was also an important road and rail junction. The towns of Bruree and Bruff are north and north-west of Kilmallock, and capturing and holding these towns was crucial to the defence of Kilmallock.[25]

The town of Kilmallock nestles in a depression on the banks of the River Lubach. It is overlooked on the north, the east and the south-west by three hills: Kilmallock Hill, Ash Hill and Quarry Hill. All these hills are within one kilometre of the town and control the approaches. If these hills could be held, the capture of the town by pro-Treaty forces would be very difficult.

The republicans seized their opportunity while the battle for Limerick was raging, and captured the Free State barracks at Kilmallock.[26] The *Freeman's Journal* of 24 July elaborates:

> On Wednesday night, July 12th, at 9.20 p.m. the town of Kilmallock was invested by Irregulars and the troops at the Union barracks were cut off from communication with the outside. The garrison of forty-nine men ... held out for forty-eight hours and finally yielded, having only a small supply of ammunition left.

Ashill Towers, a large mansion on Ash Hill, became the republican headquarters at Kilmallock. On 15 July pro-Treaty Commandant S. Ó hÓgáin confirmed that while:

> Lynch has moved his headquarters from Limerick city to Clonmel, the situation in East and West Limerick is not good. Caherconlish and Kilmallock were taken by the enemy on 13th inst. Both posts were weak and weakly garrisoned and it was a mistake to have held them.[27]

Despite capturing Kilmallock, the republicans were experiencing some difficulties. An urgent dispatch was sent to O/C 1st Southern Division on 16 July: 'Supplies very scarce here – no meat whatsoever. A daily supply is necessary. Some bedding also necessary. Philpot the QM has list of requirements. Am about to proceed to Ashill Towers with view to taking it over. Prisoners taken this morning being sent to Buttevant. C.O.B.'[28]

The loss of Kilmallock left the pro-Treaty forces in the area in a particularly weak position. Eoin O'Duffy confirmed this weak position, noting that the pro-Treaty troops 'held only Rockbarton and Bruff in that county', and estimating 'the total strength of the republicans in the county, including the city, as 2,030 rifles'.[29] Neeson suggests that the terrain and the fact that the area was occupied by veteran, disciplined soldiers from the War of Independence, with fresh troops from the south and west, and supply lines and communications that could not be easily cut gave the republicans a considerable advantage.[30] However, as in Limerick, there again appears to have been little overall direction from republican leaders in the Kilmallock area. Hopkinson quotes Adjutant-General Con Maloney telling Ernie O'Malley that 'Deasy is more or less O/C operations', and that the O/C of the Limerick brigade reported that the East Limerick column 'refused to operate under Cork'.[31] He also quotes Seán Murray of Cork No. 1 brigade recording that 'they had to scrounge for themselves', and that Deasy admitted that they had to demobilise men because they could not feed them.[32] Dissension among the leaders and quarter-mastering difficulties were not conducive to strengthening republican morale. In stark contrast, O'Duffy and General W.R.E. Murphy – who had been a lieutenant-colonel in the British army – formed a resolute unified command, and Murphy, 'whose mind was still conditioned by his experience of trench warfare', prepared detailed plans 'for an attack on the ancient town of Kilmallock'.[33]

On the night of Sunday 23 July, the hitherto successful pro-Treaty troops, when pursuing the republicans retreating south from Limerick, were abruptly checked at Ballycullane Cross about a mile north of Kilmallock. The 'Irish Republican Army Official Bulletin' in the *Cork Examiner* of 25 July reported that 'at 3.20 a.m. on Sunday morning there was a sharp engagement … in the vicinity of Ballycullane Cross. After a brief fight the Free State troops were defeated. One Free State soldier was killed and … four prisoners, four rifles … and a quantity of war equipment' was captured. On the same evening, at Thomastown, south-west of Kilmallock, the Free State forces suffered another reverse. Frank O'Connor, a republican correspondent, stirringly recounts the incident in the 'Irish Republican Army Official Bulletin' in the *Cork Examiner* of 26 July:

On my way back to Kilmallock, I, my driver and a member of the Ambulance Corps ... were arrested by a column of Free State troops. These had occupied a farmer's house by the roadside and there we were taken and placed in a small dirty room where we found three other prisoners. After three or four hours we were ordered out ... when suddenly a shout of 'boys we are surrounded' was raised. A fierce outburst of firing startled our guards ... and we were ordered to stretch ourselves on the ground. Our position in the small room became more desperate ... one of the garrison in the upper loft was killed ... O'Mahony of Blarney St, Cork ... many of them had no heart in the fighting and appealed to their officers to surrender ... shortly afterwards the officer in charge was shot through the mouth, and as he fell, men threw out the white flag and shouted surrender. The principal impression which the encounter with the Free Staters left in my mind was the utter lack of conviction that makes the republicans fight like demons.

Propaganda aside, defeat in these initial contacts with the republican forces must have been a serious setback for the pro-Treaty columns. These reverses were further compounded when pro-Treaty HQ, 4th Southern Division Rockbarton, reported on 24 July that 'Comdt Cronin, with forty-seven men, were captured near Thomastown after an engagement with Irregulars which from reports seems to have been of five hours duration'. This may be the same action reported by O'Connor above. However, a further defeat was reported in the same dispatch:

On the evening of the 24th inst. a detachment of Comdt Cronin's column at Ballingaddy advanced towards the enemy's outposts ... were compelled to retire ... Lieut O'Leary and three men were captured by the enemy. Three of these men were found shot dead on the road this morning near the enemy post and it is believed they were shot after surrender.[34]

This pro-Treaty allegation of a republican atrocity is contradicted by an eyewitness account quoted by Neeson. The witness noticed 'four soldiers crouched at the bottom of a bank' hoping that republican 'machine-gunners didn't see them'. However 'a burst tore through them, killing three and fatally wounding the fourth.' The next day, 'a Red Cross party went through the anti-Treaty lines … under a flag of truce'. They were 'received with courtesy by the well-armed and well disciplined men', and were allowed to retrieve the bodies 'where they had been laid out with their Rosary beads in their hands'.[35]

These republican successes are corroborated by documents in the Siobhán Lankford papers in the Cork Archives. Terse republican reports of 'daily operations' in the Kilmallock area on 23 and 24 July state that fifty-eight prisoners, sixty rifles, 2,000 rounds of .303 ammunition, along with other sundry war materials were captured with minimal republican losses.[36]

The opening skirmishes in this region were clearly going in favour of the defending republicans, and, as reported in the *Cork Examiner* of 27 July, 'the Free State forces were completely repulsed'.[37] However, what was important for the pro-Treaty forces was that, despite relatively heavy losses, they had established the whereabouts of the republican defensive outposts around Kilmallock.

Both sides believed that possession of the towns of Bruff and Bruree were crucial to the fate of Kilmallock. The republicans made a serious attempt to capture Bruff on 20 July. The *Freeman's Journal* reported that early on the morning of Thursday 20 July, while inspecting outposts, pro-Treaty officers made contact with attacking republican forces: 'Almost immediately a band of thirty Irregulars suddenly emerged from a house and joined in the attack.' They advanced from the south and surrounded the barracks on all sides, and 'torrents of machine-gun and rifle fire, punctuated by the explosion of hand grenades broke the stillness of the morning'. During the fight, the republicans made determined efforts to capture the town. They seized 'the Munster and Leinster and National Banks and adjoining cottages', although early in the encounter 'an Irregular leader was severely wounded in the chest.' The attack continued into Friday morning, when after 10 a.m. 'a calm set in and the Irregulars made towards Rockbarton with the evident intention of attacking the National garrison'.[38] On 20 July, republican field GHQ at Ashill Towers referred to the Bruff attack reporting to O/C 1st Southern:

> At 3 a.m. this morning columns 6 and 7 entered Bruff and took up positions on the east, west and south sides of the Free State barracks. As they were entering, a sharp engagement took place, in which Comdt Tom O'Connor of the 6th Battn Kerry No. 2 brigade got seriously wounded through the left shoulder … the enemy is practically surrounded. No. 5 column is keeping Rockbarton engaged so as to keep off reinforcements from that side.[39]

However, the report does not mention the failure of the assault as was claimed in the pro-Treaty account in the *Freeman's Journal*. Despite the tenacious defence described in this account, republicans were determined to capture the town and on 23 July, the anti-Treatyites again attacked Bruff, captured it and established a field hospital just outside the town, adding to the woes of the pro-Treaty forces.[40]

Despite the initial success of the republicans in Bruff, the tide was beginning to turn slightly in favour of the pro-Treaty forces. They retook Bruff on Sunday 30 July. From this position they decided to launch a counter-attack on Bruree, having evacuated their position there three days previously. Neeson states that 'the pro-Treatyites decided that Bruree must be captured' and, indeed, held 'before Kilmallock could be attacked'. He explains that 'Bruff, which had again changed hands was used as the springboard from which to launch the attack' to retake Bruree.[41] This assault was launched on 30 July. In the 'Irish Republican Army Official Bulletin' in the *Cork Examiner*, it was stated that 'the attack was made on Bruree by a Free State force numbering about 300, supported by two armoured cars and several machine-guns.'[42] A republican report to the chief-of-staff in Fermoy elaborates:

> At 7.30 p.m. last night an advance was made on Bruree by Free State forces numbering approx. 300 being supported by three armoured cars and several machine-guns. A small section of our men numbering about twelve were occupying Bruree and railway bridge convenient. Due to Lewis gun fire they found it impossible to hold the bridge and had to withdraw. Scouts at Clogheen Hill had been surrounded and taken prisoner. Lost twelve men, eleven rifles and one Lewis gun.

The seriousness of the tactical loss of Bruree for the republicans is emphasised in an addendum to the report, where the officer says, 'as yet I have not received a report of this catastrophe'.[43] However, the republican outer defences around Kilmallock were holding. A republican report states that during a general 'advance on our lines all along east to Bulgaden … at Ballygubba Cross' two miles north west of Kilmallock, 'a party of enemy troops came in contact with our forces. Four killed and the rest surrendered. Thirteen rifles and one Lewis gun captured by our forces. The enemy failed to break through our lines.'[44] However, the *Freeman's Journal* of 31 July reports the comments of General O'Duffy, GOC South-Western Division Command, who was in a bullish mood:

> I am well pleased by the progress made by the troops. In this command the best fighting material the Irregulars can muster is ranged against us … on the west we occupied Croom yesterday and today Bruree … I consider the capture of Bruree of much strategic value, making Kilmallock untenable.[45]

The consequences of defeat at Bruree were not lost on the republican leadership. Yet Neeson argues that 'minor clashes' in the hinterland of Kilmallock 'indicated that, far from preparing to evacuate Kilmallock, the anti-Treatyites were jockeying for position around it'.[46] The *Freeman's Journal* reports that 'on 31 July the National Garrison in the Rectory on the outskirts of Kilmallock was attacked by a large force of Irregulars', and following a 'brave resistance the garrison was forced to yield'.[47] A second attack was made at another 'unoccupied house held by Free State forces, using an armoured car, a Lewis gun, a Maxim gun and a Thompson gun'. Understandably, with such firepower the republicans 'scattered the occupying force, capturing eight prisoners, twelve rifles, one Lewis gun, ammunition and rifle grenades'.[48] This republican offensive – planned by Deasy and Seán Moylan – was aimed at capturing Patrickswell, recapturing Bruree, re-establishing dominance in south Limerick and protecting their headquarters at Kilmallock.[49]

The town of Patrickswell is situated fifteen miles north of Bruree and on the main road west to north Kerry. The town controlled the traffic to the west and also provided cover for strategically important Bruree. Patrickswell was 'attacked and captured' by the republicans 'on 2 August and preceded by only a few hours the large-scale counter-attack on Bruree'.[50] On the same day, a republican force with 'two armoured cars left Ashill Towers to attack Bruree with two columns'.[51] The pro-Treaty South-Western Command daily report states that:

> Bruree was attacked at 6.30 a.m. by a force estimated at 500 men. The Dublin Guards under Commandant Flood formed the garrison. The Irregulars used two armoured lorries and a trench mortar. They attacked the outpost under Capt. Dinan ... and after two hours fighting, fifteen of our forces were taken prisoner. Comdt Flood drove off the Irregulars at all other points. There was a serious attempt made to

capture Bruree House using Thompson, Lewis guns and rifle grenades.[52]

The report also recounts how pro-Treaty reinforcements arrived from Limerick with the armoured car known as 'The Custom House', and relieved the beleaguered Bruree garrison. Having failed to capture the strong-point, Bruree House, the republicans 'withdrew when enemy forces arrived with overwhelming numbers'.[53] The failure to recapture Bruree was a serious blow to the republicans, whilst boosting pro-Treaty morale, and 'was the beginning and the end of [any] anti-Treaty offensive'.[54] Failure to capture Bruree also made the tactical capture of Patrickswell irrelevant, and on 3 August, after only twenty-four hours in occupation, the republicans withdrew from the town.[55] At this stage, pro-Treaty dominance of all areas north of Kilmallock finally exposed the republican stronghold to an assault on all sides, planned by the pro-Treaty leaders for 4 August 1922.

General Murphy's plan to seize Kilmallock, Operation Order No. 6,[56] was issued at 3 p.m. on 3 August 1922 to all officers commanding forces involved in the attack. The orders were as follows:

- The Irregulars will be attacked along the whole front from Adare to Kilmallock at 6 a.m., 4 August 1922.
- Col Commandant Keogh will attack Adare at 6 a.m. from the east.
- O/C West Limerick brigade (Brigadier Keane) will attack Adare at 6 a.m. from the south.
- Commandant Flood will leave a section (twenty-five men) in Bruree. They will act as garrison and flank guard. With the remainder of his men he will attack and establish an entrenched position on Knocksouna Hill.
- Captain Casey, commanding the Limerick City brigade detachment, will move on Commandant Flood's left flank and prolong the attack in the direction of Tankardstown.
- Comdt General Galvin will move one hundred men to

the Forge Cross at Ballymuddagh. They will attack Ballygubba at 6 a.m. from the left flank and the direction of the
attack will be from the east.

- Captain Dominick with his Coy will attack and capture
the hill known as Dalton's Hill, and advance on the west
side of Kilmallock. He will clear the Irregulars from Ash
Hill Towers [*sic*].
- Commandant General Galvin will attack with 120 men
Grange Hill. When the position is cleared, this will clear
Kilmallock and form line on S.W. of the town.
- Commandant General Galvin will arrange to attack with
fifty men westwards along the railway. They will act in co-
operation with the force attacking Ash Hill Towers.
- Commandant General Hannigan will collect one hundred
men, and station them at the crossroads south of Green-
park House. They will be used as a reserve.
- The pursuit must be rapid and unceasing.
- The field artillery gun will be in position by 5.45 a.m. The
first task will be to aid in the capture of Grange Hill and
Dalton's Hill, afterwards it will range on Ash Hill Towers.

Detailed orders were also issued for the use of the Whippet
armoured car, and the HQ centre for reports was to be at Ballycullane for Kilmallock. All officers were to acknowledge the receipt
of the orders. Murphy's detailed planning contrasts sharply with
the dissension and unrest reported by Hopkinson amongst the
republican leadership.

The strenuous efforts made to prevent pro-Treaty forces from
getting control of Bruff and Bruree must have led the attackers
to expect grim resistance from the defending republican forces
at Kilmallock. On 4 August 1922 the South-Western Command
daily report states that 'Irregulars held Kilmallock in force,
estimated at about 600 men ... and it is estimated that there are
a further 400 men between Kilmallock and Charleville'. Concern
is also expressed in the report that 'they have good railway

communication with Buttevant and Mitchelstown', and that 'their billet area extends to Kilfinnane'.[57] All these towns held by the republicans were within fifteen miles of Kilmallock. A special intelligence report issued on 4 August must have further heightened the concerns of the attacking pro-Treaty commandants. It states that 'the area one mile south and west of Kilmallock is held by 1,000 Irregulars', and that two flying columns – of seventy and fifty men respectively – operated in Tully and Ardpatrick. Referring to arms, the report says that 'they seem to be well-armed in Kilmallock with rifles and ammunition. Machine-guns and ammunition; rifle grenades; one or two armoured lorries and a plentiful supply of explosives and mines … with about twenty lorries used as transport for men and material.'[58] These estimates indicated an impending and determined republican defence of Kilmallock, with the worrying potential for overwhelming counter-attack from the south.

However, Operation Order No. 6 still held, and 'in accordance with the general scheme of operations, it was decided to attack the Irregulars' positions on the front Kilmallock–Ballygubba Cross–Bruree' as planned.[59] The attacking troops were as follows:

- 366 men of 1st Southern Division under Commandant General Galvin.
- 138 1st Dublin brigade regulars, under Captain Dominick.
- 96 Dublin Guards, under Commandant Flood.
- 60 Limerick City brigade under Flood.
- 100 East Limerick brigade were held in reserve under Colonel Commandant Scannell.[60]

In view of the estimated republican forces defending Kilmallock, 660 assault troops seemed inadequate, even though 'one 18-pounder and an armoured car accompanied the troops'.[61]

The defence of Kilmallock was based on holding the four hills overlooking the town. It was important to capture Knocksouna two miles to the west, and critical to take Ash Hill to the south-west, Kilmallock Hill to the north and Quarry Hill to the north-east. It is not surprising, then, that the objectives of the attacking forces were outlined as follows:

- To seize the hills on the north-west and north-east of Kil-mallock – thereby dominating the town.
- To push forward to Ballygubba Cross from Forge Cross establishing a straight line from Kilmallock to Knock-souna.
- To seize Knocksouna Hill, a dominating position one mile south of Bruree and overlooking the Loobagh river valley and approaches to Charleville.[62]

The narrative of Kilmallock operations recounts the progression of the pro-Treaty attack:

The assembly was completed at 6.30 a.m. Owing to the artillery not having reconnoitred the positions assigned to them, a delay of two hours was occasioned. The attack then started at 8.30 a.m., the signal being the firing of the first shell at Strafford's, a house immediately in front of the 1st Southern Division's assembly position and known to be a machine-gun post. Two machine-gun posts – 'Strafford's' and 'Walsh's' – were shelled, and the infantry advanced. Thompson and rifle fire was opened on the 1st Southern but no casualties were sustained.

The attack 1st Brigade Dublin Regulars was carried out rapidly and the first real resistance was encountered on the slopes of Kilmallock Hill. Heavy fire from Thompson and rifles made progress slow from that point. Captain Dominick then extended his flank to the east and advanced on the hill from two directions, east and north. The armoured car was then brought into action, and the artillery brought to bear on the Irregulars in the quarries. Fox's Mount, a house on the hill, was then taken and half the hill was in our hands. Five casualties were sustained, all slightly wounded.

In the meantime the attack on Quarry Hill on the east progressed slowly. The officers of the 1st Southern did not grip their men and push them on from position to position. This was done for them and their unit brought up into line. A gap between the 1st Southern and Dublin Regulars was filled by the East Limerick brigade detachment under Col Commandant Scannell. Quarries on this front were shelled and the local inhabitants state they believe the Irregulars suffered severe casualties.

The line having now been reformed (12.30 p.m.) at the foot of the Quarry and Kilmallock Hills, it remained to clear their positions. A general advance was ordered. A heavy burst of fire was opened on the Irregulars from cottages on Kilmallock Hill, and a barricade of a steamroller with a mine in front was encountered. While pulling the wires out of the mine a concentrated burst of fire swept the party engaged in this work, but no casualties resulted. The barricade was removed and the armoured car advanced followed closely by the infantry. The crest of the hill was thus cleared. Sniping and Thompson fire still came from a cluster of houses on the main Bruff–Kilmallock road. The 18-pounder silenced this fire and our infantry occupied the position. By 3.30 p.m. we had established a cordon on all the heights overlooking the town. A mutual sniping contest followed. Our positions were then consolidated, and it was decided that, owing to the fatigue of the men, the task of clearing the remainder of the town would be postponed till morning.

At Ballygubba our troops engaged the enemy from the east and after a brisk engagement of an hour's duration, succeeded in capturing the positions. The Dublin Guards, under Commandant Flood, advanced on Knocksouna, meeting with but a feeble resistance, and occupied entrenched posts on this hill. Long-range sniping with Thompson guns ensued, but no casualties were sustained. A detachment of Limerick City brigade garrisoned Bruree during the advance.

On 5/8/22 at 8.30 a.m. Kilmallock was entered by our troops. Eight prisoners (four with arms), an ambulance and a quantity of ammunition were captured. Mines were removed and roads cleared. All bridges, buildings etc. were intact. An outpost line from Kilmallock westwards along Tankardstown and Knocksouna ridges was established.

Our casualties were one killed, eight wounded. Enemy's casualties not known, but six coffins were commandeered by them and according to locals, about thirty-nine were wounded. Reports also put the enemy's strength at 500 to 700.[63]

On the face of it, General Murphy's plan worked perfectly. The republican stronghold of Kilmallock was captured with minimal casualties on the pro-Treaty side, especially considering the number and quality of the forces ranged against them. Neeson explains that what Murphy 'did not know was that the bulk of the anti-Treaty defenders had succeeded in withdrawing – past Flood on Knocksouna Hill – before the first assault was launched'.[64] The pro-Treaty *Freeman's Journal* reported that:

From six o'clock till midnight on Friday 4 July the National encampment was assailed on all sides by roving bands of Irregulars who made surprise sorties on our outposts … they put up a stiff fight … the enemy fell back but kept up an intermittent fire until close on dawn.[65]

These attacks were 'a screen behind which the evacuation took place. Their job had been to fight a rearguard action while the remainder of the garrison withdrew.'[66] The Kerry brigades who fought in Limerick and Kilmallock had been ordered to withdraw because 'on August 2nd, three days before Kilmallock was cleared, Dublin Guards under the command of General Patrick Daly landed at Fenit on the north side of Tralee Bay'.[67] For the Kerry republicans, defence of the kingdom of Kerry took precedence over protection of the 'Republic of Munster'.

3

Retreat to North Cork

RETREAT FROM KILMALLOCK

The capture of Kilmallock on 5 July 1922 was a major factor contributing to the fall of the northern half of the 'Republic of Munster'. The hasty retreat southwards of the republican forces and their unwillingness to engage with the pro-Treaty army is not easy to explain. They had shown their mettle in Limerick and in the engagements prior to the fall of Kilmallock. It is difficult to understand why these republican troops, led by battle-hardened officers, with plentiful war materials in their possession, did not make a stand at another easily defended strong-point or why they failed to harry the advancing pro-Treaty forces. An effective engagement would have weakened pro-Treaty forces, delayed their unopposed sweep through Counties Limerick and Cork, given republicans time to regroup, and – above all – would have raised flagging republican morale.

Florrie O'Donoghue suggests that the capacity of the republicans 'to retain control of south Munster was nullified' by Free State 'use of coastwise shipping to land troops at strategic points',[1] and this must have been a major factor in the republican retreat. In Waterford, the landing of reinforcements, arms and ammunition from the armed trawler *Helga* to support General Prout's pro-Treaty forces contributed to the fall of the city. However, Michael Hopkinson asserts that the ease which with Waterford was captured 'is explained more by republican failure than by the effectiveness of the strategy adopted by Provisional Government troops'. He quotes sources alleging that republican forces were 'in a state of tension' and that 'desertion was frequent'.[2] Commandant Pax Whelan reported that there was 'a serious situation' in the brigade because 'two of the most important officers have sent in their resignations', and furthermore mentioned a serious shortage of guns and ammunition.[3] Another problem was that a column under Commandant Pa Murray making its way from Cork to support the defenders inexplicably did not reach Waterford in time. Also – and crucially – the planned attack on the rear of the pro-Treaty forces by Tipperary republicans led by two of the most celebrated War of Independence commandants, Dinny Lacey and Dan Breen, failed to materialise.[4]

Landings by sea of pro-Treaty troops coupled with a clear lack of coordinated effective command structures and serious problems with morale were major factors contributing to the collapse of republican forces in Waterford and the consequent retreat from the south-east. With Limerick and Waterford captured, pro-Treaty forces were now free to roll up the ends of the republican defensive line, press forward aggressively, and eliminate isolated pockets of republican resistance. Republican defeat at Waterford presaged 'the fall of Carrick-on-Suir after a three day struggle', the capture of Golden 'in a surprise attack', and the evacuation of Tipperary town.[5]

Subsequent landings of pro-Treaty forces were made at Fenit, County Kerry, on 2 August, and at Passage West, County Cork, on 8 August with further landings in County Cork along the coast at Youghal and Union Hall. These landings precipitated the same domino republican collapse in these counties as had happened in Waterford.[6] When a landing was made in County Kerry, at Kenmare, pro-Treaty forces 'quickly captured the town, the Irregulars having quickly decamped'.[7] Having landed at Fenit, Free State troops under Brigadier Patrick O'Daly 'pushed on to Tralee and in the following days occupied Castleisland, Listowel and Farranfore'.[8]

At Rochestown and Douglas, County Cork, Free State troops

under Emmet Dalton for once met stiff, sustained resistance from the republican forces. Despite this, on 9 August 'Dalton made his assured way into Cork',[9] while, in sharp contrast, 'the republican forces, in extreme and confused haste, evacuated the city, hardly having time for the obligatory burning of barracks'.[10] Dalton, having captured Cork, referred to the republican exit, stating in amazement: 'It is hard to credit the extent of the disorder and disorganisation that was displayed in the retreat.'[11] On the opposing side Pa Murray, one of the most effective of Cork column leaders, commented: 'When we left Cork city I thought the whole thing was finished.' Hopkinson asserts that at this stage Pa Murray also told Liam Lynch that 'this was the time to end the war.'[12]

In north Munster, the pro-Treaty forces were advancing just as rapidly, and in most cases meeting only token resistance. Adare was evacuated by republicans on 5 August, and on 7 August 'Newcastle West was entered by the National Army ... after a twelve hour battle, in the course of which ten Irregulars were killed', having advanced 'from Rathkeale at 3 o'c. that morning'.[13] Coastal landings of pro-Treaty troops were another factor in the republican retreat in north Munster. The landing of troops on the south and south-west coasts of Munster meant that republican forces were being outflanked or in danger of attack on two fronts. However, further reasons must be sought for the headlong republican retreat, since the pro-Treaty advances were made by troops described by O'Duffy in a report to Mulcahy on 4 August as 'a disgruntled, undisciplined and cowardly crowd' who 'handed over arms wholesale to the enemy'; 'the divisional, brigade, battalion and company officers were in many cases, no better than the privates.'[14]

PRO-TREATY OCCUPATION OF NORTH CORK TOWNS

After the tactical orderly evacuation of Kilmallock, the republican

retreat southwards from County Limerick gathered pace, and the flight from southern towns continued. The *Freeman's Journal* of 7 August reported that 'with the fall of Kilmallock … the Irregulars had flown southwards towards Charleville'.[15] The same issue suggested that the republicans might make a stand at Charleville and this is confirmed in the *Cork Examiner* of 25 August:

> Some time before the evacuation, preparations for a siege were made by the Irregulars on an extensive scale. Two large bridges spanning the railway line between Charleville and Kilmallock were blown up, trees were felled and other obstructions placed across the roads. Sandbag fortifications were placed outside the entrance of Madden's Imperial Hotel and the premises of Mr P.J. Ball … were utilised for hospital purposes. Mines were placed on the road opposite the police barracks at Lisnagry.

All available motor vehicles were seized and 'food and clothing was commandeered'. Fortunately for the people of Charleville, 'evacuation took place without the battle which was anticipated'.[16] Instead, the republicans retreated to Buttevant, the headquarters of Cork No. 4 brigade under Commandant Paddy O'Brien of Liscarroll. A detachment of Free State troops 'under Commandant General Denis Galvin occupied Charleville unopposed on 12 August'.[17]

Free State aerial reconnaissance added to the difficulties of the retreating republican troops. On 13 August Pilot Commandant Russell reported:

> The main road between Charleville and Mallow is absolutely clear with the exception of a trench at Woodpark. The main road from Kanturk to Charleville via Freemount was also apparently clear. (Observed from one hundred feet twice.) Bridges were observed to be blown up including the railway bridge crossing Blackwater at Mallow. Machine-gun posts:

One located half mile north of Mallow on the west side of the main road. Heavy fire from this position. Concentrations: about twenty men in farmhouse 1.75 miles N.W. of Buttevant. Some rifle shots.[18]

With this accurate, detailed, up-to-the-minute intelligence, the Free State troops pressed on southwards. Again, they met only minor resistance. Near Charleville, 'they encountered a band of Irregulars in a touring car. The Irregulars fled on the approach of the troops and abandoned the car.' Nearer to Buttevant, a detachment of Dublin Guards 'encountered a party of Irregulars caught in the act of mining the road. Eleven of the party were captured with their motorcar and a large quantity of mines and explosives.'[19] The *Freeman's Journal* of 15 August reported that the town of Buttevant had been evacuated by the republicans 'after burning all the buildings that might be of any service to the National Army'. Inevitably 'Comdt Flood's Company occupied Buttevant on the 15th inst'[20] and installed themselves in whatever buildings escaped destruction. The ease with which they occupied these towns must have baffled the Free State troops, given the known numbers and quality of the republican troops in the locality.

While Flood was advancing south, Commandant Galvin was driving south-west. On 15 August 1922 he sent a dispatch to GOC SW Command Limerick stating:

> We entered Liscarroll at 10 p.m. and succeeded in capturing twelve prisoners, including O/C Cork No. 4 brigade (M. Brislane) and his principal supporters. The roads between Charleville and Liscarroll are badly damaged. Enemy forces are still around the area. We would want a supply of ammunition and grenades for rifle. Food is very scarce here. Troops without rations.[21]

Mick Brislane was in fact commandant of the Charleville battalion of Cork No. 4 brigade.

However, Galvin's force did not have it all their own way. He reported that 'we were ambushed at 4.30 p.m. at Dromin [*sic*] midway between Liscarroll & Charleville. After three hours we were able to clear enemy and advanced to Liscarroll. It would be important to occupy Dromin as it would link us up with Charleville and break enemy communications.'[22] This delay – due to sniping – was confirmed in a republican report from 3rd battalion to brigade HQ: when entering Dromina, Free State troops 'were sniped [at] by two men … [and] held them up for two hours there'.[23] Galvin pressed on relentlessly and reported on 16 August:

> I entered Kanturk last night at twelve midnight. The Irregulars retreated some hours before our entry. We made four prisoners including the famous Seán McGrath, who is Seán Moylan's Divisional Adjutant … the lines of communication are still cut, all the roads leading here are still trenched and bridges broken. Railway line is out in places between Kanturk and Mallow.[24]

In three days, Galvin's column had covered over fifteen miles through the republican heartland, traversing broken bridges and trenched roads. No ambush had been laid to hinder its progress. Galvin had occupied two towns and at least two villages, whilst meeting only minor sniper resistance on one occasion. Republican resistance seems to have totally collapsed in the area.

Having evacuated Clonmel, republican CIC Liam Lynch had set up his headquarters in Fermoy. Florrie O'Donoghue relates how 'on 11th August Fermoy barracks was evacuated and burned',[25] and to compound matters for republicans, pro-Treaty forces, having captured Mitchelstown, reported entering Mallow on Tuesday 15 August; 'not a shot was fired and the last of the Irregulars … beating a hasty retreat from the town'.[26] The *Freeman's*

Journal quoted the pro-Treaty Publicity Department Field GHQ South-Western Command confirming that troops under Brigadier O'Daly had captured Rathmore on 17 August, and that Kanturk and Newmarket had also been occupied by the Free State troops. The same paper reported that on 18 August, 'Macroom was captured by General Dalton's forces', and that Millstreet was occupied 'by troops under Brigadier O'Daly' assisted by 'General Galvin, converging on the town from the east'.[27] Con Meaney, O/C Millstreet battalion, confirmed the occupation of Millstreet to O/C 1st Southern Division on 19 August 1922: 'The Free Staters did not get into the town until Thursday evening. Their strength is estimated from 500 to 700. Galvin and Paddy Daly are in charge.' Morale must have been low in the Millstreet battalion since Meaney reported that 'the column has been demobilised and all the arms dumped. At present there are only sixteen rifles and one Thompson in the area. I think it will be possible to bring off a few small jobs in the area.'[28] By this point, pro-Treaty forces in their dramatic sweep south and south-west from Limerick and Kilmallock between 4 August and 19 August, had occupied every significant town and village in north Munster.

REPUBLICANS REVERT TO GUERRILLA WARFARE

Superficially, this litany of pro-Treaty successes looked like a complete rout of republican forces in Munster, and particularly in North Cork. The successes seemed to herald the possibility of imminent republican defeat. Indeed, the special correspondent of the *Irish Times* concluded just that in the issue dated 15 August, saying that if the pro-Treaty forces moved quickly, the war could be over in three weeks. However, the pro-Treaty leadership was probably unaware that republican policy had been changed, and orders had been issued to vacate the towns to avoid the type of fixed defensive situation that had proved counterproductive in Kilmallock. The republican Southern Divisional O/C, Liam Deasy, issued the following order on 12 August 1922: 'As a result of the enemy invading the divisional area in numbers much larger than our available armed forces, verbal instructions to vacate all barracks and form into columns are hereby confirmed. Only the very best and most experienced men. Maximum strength of the column thirty-five men.'[29] Deasy does not say who issued the earlier 'verbal instructions'. If local commandants were issuing orders to evacuate barracks, it is possible that communication or command problems were widespread in republican ranks. CIC Liam Lynch confirmed this with Operation Order No. 9 dated 19 August: 'Our troops will now be formed into ASUs [active service units] and operate in the open.' The order specified the configuration and modus operandi of the columns in all areas.[30] Detailed instructions included the following: 'Attack or destroy if possible small enemy outposts, concentrate on destroying enemy intelligence service, attack enemy wherever he leaves his base, destroy enemy rail and road communications, intensify campaign in cities and towns.'[31] Divisional Adjutant Con Maloney added an interesting rider to Operation Order No. 9: whether to alleviate the burden on their supporters or to intimidate Free State supporters, he ordered that 'as far as possible AS Units should be billeted in mansions [that are] the property of persons hostile to the Republic.'[32]

Liam Deasy's order may explain in some way the haste with which the republicans evacuated towns after 12 August. However, it does not explain the inability or unwillingness of republican forces to confront the pro-Treaty army during the previous eight days' headlong retreat.

Because they had evacuated cities, towns and villages, the republicans had of necessity 'become a guerrilla army without barracks or bases, stores or supply services'.[33] As in the War of Independence, they were again totally dependent on the loyalty of their supporters in their areas of operation.[34] Florrie O'Donoghue outlines how, despite the loss of 'the larger towns and villages' in north and south Munster, republicans were still in control of the countryside and that 'substantial areas of the country were untouched', remaining free of Free State troops.[35] Hopkinson agrees with this assessment and quotes a pro-Treaty general report of 22 August:

> The Irregulars in Cork and Kerry are still more or less intact. Our forces have captured towns, but they have not captured Irregulars and arms on anything like a large scale, and, until this is done, the Irregulars will be capable of guerrilla warfare … Our present dispositions leave us particularly exposed to guerrilla warfare … Our forces are scattered all over the command area … it is easy to isolate our posts.[36]

The republicans, though on the run, were ominously still fully armed and undefeated, and 'guerrilla warfare tactics were to prove much more difficult to deal with than the republicans' ineffective hold on the towns had been.'[37]

For some republicans, the shift to guerrilla warfare was welcome, in that many senior officers were expert at this type of fighting and chafed at defending static positions. After all, they were now in a military situation quite similar to that of the War of Independence. However, Florrie O'Donoghue outlines differences 'of sufficient weight to be significant' when compared to conditions existing in the war against the British. He correctly assesses that 'the majority of the people were no longer with them'.[38] This was evident for quite some time before the outbreak of the Civil War. There was a countrywide sigh of relief when the Truce was declared in July 1921. The *Cork Examiner*, in its issues dated 12, 20 and 29 December, outlined the support of Cardinal Logue, republican-minded Archbishop Mannix and thirteen other Irish bishops for the Treaty. Episcopal and clerical opinion held great weight with the populace as a whole at that time. The *Cork Examiner* of 5 January 1922 confirmed the 'Strong Ratification Tide' in support of the Treaty among public bodies throughout the country, reporting that 322 public bodies had declared in favour of the Treaty, with only five against. Moreover, the election results of June 1922 demonstrated a considerable pro-Treaty majority.[39]

O'Donoghue admits that because of this pro-Treaty wave of opinion, the republicans 'felt the hostility of a large section of the people amongst whom they moved'.[40] This hostility had consequences not generally experienced during the War of Independence. In his notebooks, Ernie O'Malley says, 'in the Tan war you would be received into any house you went into, but in the Civil War you had to be very sure of your house'. He further states, 'in the Tan war, even if the area was 50 per cent against you, they would be all right. Now you had to move by night and you had to change your habits.'[41] Attitudes ranging from hostility to apathy towards republican objectives are confirmed in a garbled and bitter communication to the O/C 1st Southern Division dated 22 August 1922:

> Propaganda among the general public will not be very effective at present. Even when our army held the south intact the people did not support our side with the prospect of victory. They will not be with us now either, not so much because they are against our ideals, but because they are anxious for peace, and it is a disheartening situation for those who have wholeheartedly supported the republican army during the terror to find that in the hour of victory those on whom we most relied turned their arms viciously against their former comrades in traitorous combat for treacherous imperial arms and personal considerations regardless of the nation. It will take public conscience some time to realise the depth of their iniquity just as it did after 1916. The more they feel the pinch of war and economic pressure the sooner they will call for peace. There is nothing for it now but to keep steadily on.

> Any talk even about an accommodation only weakens us.
> SMcC.[42]

O'Donoghue also reports that, somewhat astonishingly, over 1,000 republican prisoners were taken in the first month of the Civil War. He suggests that a major factor governing the capture of republicans was that their opponents 'had an intimate and detailed knowledge of their personnel which the British lacked completely' and inevitably they knew their trusted haunts.[43]

O'Donoghue states that morale 'suffered in an atmosphere that was new to many who had not served in columns against the British'.[44] Many of the republicans had joined the IRA during the Truce and had no experience of the hardships involved in guerrilla warfare. Moreover, when they had joined the IRA they had been lionised by an admiring public, many of whom now supported the Free State and had turned against the republican forces. Low republican morale is confirmed in a pro-Treaty dispatch to Field General HQ of 22 August 1922: 'Generally the morale of the Irregulars is low. The officers are driving their men and Deasy in particular is the force behind the Irregulars in Cork.'[45] The conditions under which they had been training during the Truce period resulted in a mentality that was irked by the absence of regular quarters, decent meals and ordinary amusements. O'Donoghue added that 'many men faced the altered conditions with no great enthusiasm'.[46] For many, the changed conditions were simply too much. Liam Deasy admitted that 'many of the men just returned to their homes' and Seán O'Faolain stated bleakly that 'there was nothing left for the majority of them to do but to scatter, go into hiding, slip back at night into the city like winter foxes'.[47]

In straitened circumstances, effective reorganisation and re-motivation of officers and men was essential. O'Donoghue states that CIC Liam Lynch worked with feverish energy to encourage maximum effort and efficiency. His leadership was partially successful, to the extent that Adjutant General Con Maloney could report on 5 September that 'things have righted themselves … we have got down again to guerrilla tactics and have fallen into our stride'.[48]

However, despite Maloney's optimism, 'many republicans embarked on the guerrilla stage of the conflict with little hope of success'. In Cork, two prominent leaders, Seán O'Hegarty and Florrie O'Donoghue, chose to remain neutral and 'several of the leaders felt that an end should have been called after the fall of Cork city'.[49] Lynch reiterated republican policy: 'It is necessary to state that our national policy is to maintain the established Republic … we're finished with compromise or negotiations unless based on recognition of the Republic.' Lynch believed in military dominance at this stage, saying 'as you are already aware we have no notion of setting up a government'. His distrust of politicians can be gauged in his statement of 30 August: 'Views and opinions of political people are not to be too seriously considered. Our aim and course are now clearly defined and cut and dried.' One of his aims was to see to it that 'in the meantime no other government will be allowed function'.[50] This negative policy, with destructive undertones, met with little sympathy, and alienated many in the small towns and prosperous areas of Munster. In this atmosphere, with no prospect of outright military victory and 'with men in columns often having to live in the most uncomfortable conditions in mountain retreats and dugouts, the highest premium was placed on determination and loyalty'.[51]

REPUBLICAN DOMINATION OF NORTH CORK

Cork No. 4 column activities fulfilled to the letter Liam Lynch's Operation Order No. 9 issued on 19 August. Between 23 and 28 August, Cork No. 4 brigade columns were 'divided into three sections, twenty-four men in each'.[52] Pro-Treaty concern at this development is evident in a report to Field GHQ on 22 August: 'The North Cork Irregulars have been withdrawn to the mountainous country between Millstreet and Castleisland. At present there is reason to believe that the Irregulars in Cork County are reorganising on a new basis.'[53] The results of republican reorganisation quickly became obvious. The pro-Treaty South-Western Command reported on 29 August 1922 that 'roving bands of Irregulars are operating between our posts. Their stronghold is around Rock Chapel–Meelin–Tullylease–Freemount.'[54] These were the reorganised columns of the republican Cork No. 4 brigade.

The republican activities included constant sniping of Free State positions, trenching and blocking roads, breaking bridges, localised attacks on Free State patrols and large-scale attacks on Free State garrisons in the larger towns. On 20 August a 'section of column took part in an ambush on FS troops at Curras, Kilbrin, where one enemy officer was killed and two wounded'. Concerted pressure was applied on the Free State position in the village of Liscarroll. On 27 August, 'republicans bombed Liscarroll schoolhouse; one of the enemy lost two fingers and part of palm of hand. Another stater wounded by a sniper of ours.'[55] On 28 August, 'Free State in Liscarroll were sniped by us', and on 29 August 'all roads leading from Kanturk to Liscarroll were held by two sections, assisted by a local company. Other sections sniped town.'[56] This pressure resulted in a minor republican success in that, on 30 August, Liscarroll was 'evacuated by enemy forces'.[57]

The *Freeman's Journal* reported that also on 20 August, republicans ambushed 'a detachment of seven men under Lieut Comdt E. Cregan … returning from Liscarroll to Kanturk on Sunday evening last'. The officer in command, Lieutenant Commandant Cregan, was seriously wounded and 'the others of the party engaged the attackers'. It is alleged in the report that 'the Irregulars set the car on fire while the wounded officer was still in it'.[58] The *Cork Examiner* of 24 August also reported the ambush, but did not confirm the alleged atrocity. A republican dispatch to O/C 1st Southern Division of 2 September includes an account of the ambush resulting in 'one officer killed, one wounded. Captured three revolvers, one rifle and one Ford car.'[59] It is unclear whether the atrocity actually happened. Pro-Treaty dispatches confirm that similar ambushes took place at the end of August. On 28 August, 'a Ford car containing one officer and two privates, travelling from Millstreet to visit Banteer outpost, was ambushed two miles from Millstreet. The Irregulars were driven off … the car was put out of action'. On 30 August, 'two lorries of troops returning from Cork … were ambushed near Millstreet … two of the Irregulars were killed … five of our troops were slightly wounded'.[60] Free State forces entrenched in the towns seemed powerless to intervene. On 8 September a pro-Treaty South-Western Command report correctly assessed the situation, stating: 'About 60 of the most dangerous Irregulars are situated in the area around Dromina S.W. of Charleville.'[61] These Irregulars were dominating the countryside and creating major difficulties for the pro-Treaty forces.

The Free State forces in the town of Kanturk were sniped at six times in the last two weeks of August. Consequently, the buildings in the town occupied by them were 'heavily sandbagged'. Barricades were 'erected across all the roads on the outskirts of the town', with armed sentries 'on guard day and night'.[62] The town, and its inhabitants, were virtually under siege. They were not alone, as is confirmed by The *Cork Examiner*: 'The residents of the large and populous districts of North Cork' were 'suffering great hardships and inconvenience'. Many of the bridges that had been wrecked by republicans and subsequently restored by the Free State forces 'have again been demolished'. The main rail line between Cork and Kerry 'has ceased for some time past' and the 'traders of Kanturk and other centres in the district have to bring their supplies by road from Cork'.[63] Nearby Banteer was also subjected to republican attack and 'was sniped from two sides with great effect' on 30 August.[64] A more serious assault on Banteer was reported by South-Western Command on 8 September: 'An attack lasting three hours was made on the Banteer post. The Irregulars were beaten off sustaining two casualties.'[65] The 'dangerous Irregulars' of Cork No. 4 brigade were operating at will, and pro-Treaty dispositions had indeed left them 'particularly exposed to guerrilla warfare'. Because pro-Treaty forces were 'scattered all over the command area', it was easy to isolate their posts and, accordingly, the republican guerrilla campaign in North Cork was becoming highly effective.[66]

During the month of September, the republican columns continued to roam across North Cork and engage in guerrilla actions with little opposition. On 1 September they destroyed 'six railway chairs on the line between Charleville and Buttevant', and on 2 September 'held up Binchy's grocery van in Ballyagran village … all supplies taken from it to feed our troops'. On 4 September they entered Kilbrin to attempt assassination of 'a certain enemy officer … likely to be there', and on 6 September they 'commandeered a motor car … went to the border of Kanturk, successfully sniped two sentries, two were wounded one since reported dead … all shops closed and streets cleared'. On 2 September two sections watched 'two roads all day for returning enemy lorries … one section fired over civilians removing blockade from road'. On 4 September they blockaded 'the main roads between Charleville and Buttevant' and 'between Buttevant and Kanturk'. On 5 September a section was 'in ambush all day for enemy lorries which had passed through that morning' and on 7 September 'on brigade orders ten men proceeded to Freemount, from thence to Ballydrachan bridge, where they held positions on Newmarket from Kanturk roads from 12 midnight till 6 a.m. Enemy did not put in an appearance.'[67] They 'captured an enemy dispatch rider in Newtownshandrum village', while on 23 September, Charleville railway signal cabin was burned by republicans.[68] On 28 September a party of pro-Treaty troops 'proceeded to Newtownshandrum ... about three miles distant'. They were attacked by 'a party of Irregulars ... and Lt Ryan was wounded'.[69] Republican dispatches confirm the skirmish, stating that the attack took place 'at Boolard Cross', Newtown, and that 'Lt Ryan' was 'wounded and since died'.[70]

It was patently clear that in North Cork in September, as 'various pro-Treaty sources admitted ... guerrilla tactics were proving successful', and the wrecking of infrastructure coupled with 'the interference with communications threatened to undermine confidence in the Provisional Government's stability'.[71] This instability was exacerbated by well-organised attacks on towns. Peter O'Farrell, in his memoirs, relates details of some of the towns for which attack plans were made. The plans were worked out at a meeting in Callaghan's of Curraglas, Newtownshandrum. At this meeting, 'attended by Liam Lynch, the division staff and Paddy O'Brien, it was decided to make surprise attacks on Charleville, Kanturk, Newmarket and Millstreet barracks. Newmarket and Charleville barracks were selected to be the first barracks attacked.'[72]

O'Farrell describes the assembly of the various columns to attack Charleville and the sense of anticlimax when the attack fizzled out. The columns approached the town, but the scouts reported that 'a solitary soldier was not to be seen on the streets', and that 'all the sentries that were to be jumped had been pulled in'. To show their capacity to strike at will, 'all the Thompson gunners from the battalions sneaked in on stockinged feet to Smith's Lane corner and blazed Madden's Hotel and the Parochial Hall [where the Free Staters were billeted]. The Staters never replied.' Following their policy of 'hit and run' guerrilla tactics, the columns then withdrew. O'Farrell describes the attack as a fiasco, and ascribes the failure to engage pro-Treaty forces to the suspicion that 'some of the Charleville members of the column had found out about the attack' and 'sneaked into town and warned their families to clear out of town'.[73] Pro-Treaty spies had also got wind of the attack – hence the absence of sentries and the withdrawal of the Free State forces to barracks.

A more determined attack was made on the town of Newmarket in the early morning of 7 September 1922. A concise report was made by the adjutant of Cork No. 4 brigade on 11 September:

> On the morning of September 7th Newmarket barracks was attacked by our troops. The attack began at twelve midnight and lasted till 6 a.m. next morning ... our troops captured four of their men together with rifles and amm. Casualties on their side unknown. Casualties on our side none. The strength of the enemy forces would be from eighty to one hundred men.

In a further report, it is stated that 'the 3rd Batt. [Charleville] AS column took part in the attack on Newmarket'.[74] The *Cork Examiner* of 12 September gives a more detailed account:

> The Irregulars, whose strength was estimated at about 400, took up several strategic positions around the barracks. The town's people were rudely awakened by the intensity of machine-gun, rifle and revolver fire. The attackers bargained on taking the barracks early in the fight ... tried to rush the building behind a smoke screen formed by setting fire to some hay, but a withering fire from the garrison drove them off. One outpost comprising four men was captured. The fight was waged with great bitterness until 7.00 on Friday morning.

The terror of one family caught in the attack sheltering in a coal hole and the state of their house after the attack is graphically described: 'One bullet penetrated into their place of refuge narrowly missing one of the children. Windows of the house were shattered to atoms, doors blown off hinges, partitions riddled, pictures smashed and every article of ware broken into fragments.' The report concluded that the Irregulars 'were so confident of success that patrols were appointed to do duty in the town during the Fair on that day'.[75]

While the columns of Cork No. 4 brigade were engaged in major attacks on towns, the ASUs of each battalion engaged in activities of a less serious nature. Table 1 lists the activities of the five battalions Cork No. 4 brigade from 13–23 October:[76]

Table 1: *Cork No. 4 brigade activities, 13–23 October 1922*

Battalion	Date	Action
1st	13 Oct. 1922	Enemy Red Cross cyclist captured.
	15 Oct. 1922	Enemy posts at Millstreet sniped, a large quantity of ammunition fired by the enemy.
2nd	14 Oct. 1922	Enemy positions at Newmarket sniped. Mails raided between Kanturk and Newmarket. Several raids carried out.
	15 Oct. 1922	Enemy positions sniped in Newmarket.
	16 Oct. 1922	Enemy positions sniped in Newmarket. The enemy replied with machine-gun fire. Volunteers B Company made large trench.
3rd	16 Oct. 1922	Telephone wires between Charleville and Buttevant cut at 7 p.m. Held up Liscarroll and Churchtown mails.
	17 Oct. 1922	Cut poles and wires on railway line between Charleville and Buttevant. Chairs on Buttevant–Charleville line destroyed. Spy notices posted. Mails from Charleville to Dromina held up and censored. Burned *Cork Examiners*. Trenches on Charleville–Dromina road, Milford and Drumcollogher road. Trench impassable at Newtownshandrum. Pony and trap seized from a farmer who refused to billet men. Drewscourt bridge demolished. Attack by 4 ASU on Charleville. Reported two dead, one mortally wounded.

	12 Oct. 1922	Fired on enemy armoured train from Buttevant to Limerick at Shannagh.
	16 Oct. 1922	Four ASU sniped Charleville. Two entered the town with their boots off. Fired on Parochial Hall (Enemy HQ)
	19 Oct. 1922	Cut poles and wires on Charleville–Bruree line and on Charleville–Dublin line. Broke insulators.
	20 Oct. 1922	636 chairs removed on line between Ballinguile bridge and Shannagh. A mile of track removed from up and down line. Poles and wires cut.
	21 Oct. 1922	Fired on breakdown gang repairing line. While prisoners being conveyed to Limerick by FS troops, fire opened on them at Shannagh.
	23 Oct. 1922	Enemy troops from Charleville surrounded Newtown. Sniped on return to Charleville.
4th		Report not to hand. Summary – demolishing bridges etc.
5th	14 Oct. 1922	Enemy party raiding houses in Mourneabbey sniped by two ASU men. Drove to Mallow at speed.
		No activities at Kilshannig for the week. Column on guard at Analeentha for officers of the 1st Southern Division.
	12–13 Oct. 1922	Ambush at Rathnee and Scart. No chance at enemy.
	17 Oct. 1922	Fired at enemy across Blackwater. Sniped guard minding crashed aeroplane.

The 3rd battalion of Cork No. 4 brigade also reported on 2 October that they had destroyed ten bridges in the vicinity of Charleville and Liscarroll, blocked the Charleville–Buttevant road and the Charleville–Doneraile road, and trenched all the roads in the area. On 5 October they reported that the mails were held up between Charleville and Liscarroll, that thirteen roads were obstructed in the area and that twenty bridges had been destroyed.[77]

The extent and intensity of the guerrilla activities must have been a severe setback to the pro-Treaty forces that had occupied the towns and villages in August with comparative ease. Free State forces occupied the town of Charleville on 12 August, but it was nineteen days later – on 31 August – before the *Cork Examiner* could report the first arrest of republicans: 'On Sunday night there was considerable military activity in the town and vicinity.' Free State forces arrested Michael Motherway, who was Chairman of the Charleville Rural District Council,[78] and some others. Whether by accident or design, a pro-Treaty note was found by a republican somewhere in Charleville on 11 September saying, 'Operations are to start immediately for a general round-up of the republicans in this district starting with Newtown. All the republican resorts [*sic*] are supposed to be known to our officers.' The note included cryptic message in parentheses: '11th Sept. Burn this!' The round-up duly took place. A report to the I/O 1st Southern Division of the IRA stated that 'four lorries and one private car arrived in Charleville from Kilmallock and after a short delay proceeded to Newtown ... Roughly 200 men took part in this coup. They arrested four civilians ... none of our men were taken as they left the locality after receiving this information.'[79] The note implies that general round-ups of republicans were not planned until mid-September. This is difficult to understand given the high level of republican activity in the area. The Free State intelligence was good, in that the haunts of the republicans were known, but it is strange that the Charleville garrison did not consider raiding Newtown prior to this, since Newtown is only five kilometres from Charleville.

STRUGGLE FOR DOMINANCE IN NORTH CORK

The Newtown search was the precursor to searches of specific areas and large-scale general sweeps of larger areas, such as neighbouring parishes where republicans were suspected to be billeted. The *Cork Examiner* of 19 September reported that 'large forces of National troops under the command of General Galvin … have been conducting sweeping movements between Kanturk, Mallow and Millstreet'. The report suggests that 'several arrests have been effected'. No names were mentioned, but in another report doubt is cast on the appropriateness of the arrest of one suspect, a Mr Dennehy of Kanturk, since he 'enjoyed a high degree of respect and popularity in this locality'.[80] Free State searches were conducted in Milford and Cooline, near Charleville, on 22 September, and Newtown on 24 September. Arrests were made on each occasion. As previously mentioned, Lieutenant Ryan was killed on 30 September in the course of a search at Boolard, Newtown,[81] and a 3rd battalion Cork No. 4 brigade report says that on 30 September 'enemy troops under Galvin were in the village of Newtown, Michael Cronin of Charleville, brother of Ed Cronin fired two revolver shots at the door of Mr Shine. On return journey sniped by three of our ASU men.'[82]

Some of these searches were nocturnal. Republicans responded by ambushing the search parties and continuing to attack Free State posts. On Wednesday 3 October, while engaged in a nocturnal search near Millstreet, 'a party of seven in a motorcar and under the command of Commandant Healy, Adjutant [Free State] 1st Cork brigade were suddenly alarmed by fire from two Thompson guns followed by rifle and rifle grenade fire.' Fire was returned, and the Free State forces tried to evade the ambush by pushing the car silently along the road. Suddenly, 'a terrific fusillade was opened … and the car was completely riddled on one side as well as the back'. Commandant Healy ordered the men to 're-enter the car', and they dashed 'through a running fire for about half a mile' and finally re-entered Millstreet.[83]

On Wednesday 10 October a successful search was made in the Ballyhea district by Charleville troops, who 'made a number of arrests'. The arrest of seven Volunteers is confirmed in a 3rd battalion report to Cork No. 4 brigade in which it is also alleged that Free State soldier 'Ml. Cronin, questioning a man named Drinan, put a revolver to his head and threatened to blow his brains out'.[84] The search party returned to barracks unchallenged.[85] However, on Tuesday 17 October 'three soldiers were wounded, two seriously', when 'Irregulars attacked the posts occupied by National troops at Charleville'. There 'was heavy firing during the course of the attack' resulting in 'some miraculous escapes'.[86]

On 14 October a flying column of National forces was ambushed at Mourneabbey. The fight lasted for three quarters of an hour. On the night of Wednesday 19 October, another party of National troops was ambushed at Castletownroche. The Irregulars – who it is stated were 200 strong – opened fire with a Thompson gun and a Peter the Painter. Fire was returned with a machine-gun and 'the Irregulars took to their heels'.[87]

Newtown was again the target for a Free State early-morning raid on 23 October. 'Five of the ASU staying in Newtownshandrum. Informed at 5.30 a.m. that enemy troops from Charleville had surrounded the village' on a 'round-up expedition'. The enemy numbered 'between eighty and one hundred men'. The section leader 'instructed his men to retreat towards Charleville and get outside enemy positions'. The republicans 'did not have anything to eat, were exhausted ... [but] took up positions on the back road to Charleville, advanced within one hundred yards range, opening fire at the same time'.[88] The *Cork Examiner* of 27 October confirms that this search took place and states that 'a youth named Shine from Newtownshandrum was captured' and that the 'Irregulars suffered severe casualties'.[89] Further Free State round-ups were carried out in late October 'in the districts of Mourneabbey and Rathduff'. Republicans raided Buttevant on 27 October, and after 'a hot engagement, which lasted till four o'clock on Thursday morning', the attackers were beaten off.[90]

The pattern of day and night searches and sweeps was well established by the end of October, but Free State forces had little success apart from the capture of some republican small fry. The Free State Command could not have been pleased with progress: they were still subject to surprise attack in the towns and they were gravely embarrassed when, on 9 October, twenty-eight republican prisoners in Kanturk 'escaped at night bringing two rifles and two hundred rds of ammunition by disarming the guard'.[91]

Hopkinson suggests that 'between September and December a kind of military stalemate existed'. Republican successes were limited to ambushes and destruction of infrastructure. The lack of observable pro-Treaty progress, however, 'reflected badly on the government'.[92] He quotes the special correspondent of the *Irish Times*, Theodore Kingsmill Moore, writing from Limerick on 20 September: 'Ever since the radical change in strategy made by the Irregulars in August, it has been increasingly difficult for the National Army to strike any blow of immediate effect.'[93] The National Army did have some minor successes, having embarked on the new policy of raids and sweeps that was recommended by Dalton when writing to Mulcahy: 'There was only one obvious course for us to take and that was to harass them and keep them moving.'[94] This policy of constant harassment would bear fruit for the pro-Treaty forces later in the year and especially in the early months of 1923. However, in the autumn of 1922, the republican forces in North Cork were on the front foot because, as Dalton admitted, 'the pro-Treaty forces allowed the republicans to regroup by not moving decisively against them',[95] and that consequently 'the republicans had won back the initiative'.[96]

The republicans of Cork No. 4 brigade were operating over territory they knew intimately, and their skilful guerrilla tactics had been well honed in the War of Independence. Their ability to carry out operations indicate that they had the support of a loyal section of the population in the hinterland, and that their commander,

Commandant Paddy O'Brien, was a skilful guerrilla leader. In North Cork, the republicans could be considered successful – if success was measured by the extent to which infrastructure was destroyed, ambushes carried out and persistent raids made on towns.

This degree of success contrasted sharply with some of the other brigades in Cork at this point. Hopkinson states that 'Cork republican IRA men very reluctantly entered the war and showed little commitment to it.'[97] Republican P.J. McHugh commented that 'the Cork men had no interest in the Civil War', while Florrie Begley declared 'we had no heart in the Civil War ... when the attack on the Four Courts was over the fight should have been stopped'.[98] Hopkinson further argues that 'many republicans embarked on the guerrilla stage of the conflict with little hope of success', and as has already been noted, some of the leaders felt that the fight should have ended with the fall of Cork city.[99]

A review of the Cork brigades was made at a divisional meeting on 30 October. It concluded: 'Cork 1 Brigade is disorganised ... Cork 3 is also in a very poor state ... Cork 4 is keeping together pretty well but the enemy are not travelling through the area except in very large numbers. Cork 5 is in a good state.'[100] In contrast, on 5 October 1922 HQ 5th battalion Cork No. 4 brigade had reported to the adjutant of Cork No. 4 that fifteen bridges had been broken in the vicinity of Mallow, all roads in the area were blocked except one, telegraph poles had been cut between Mallow and Lombardstown and between Mallow and Buttevant, the railway signal cabs had been wrecked at Mourneabbey and Lombardstown, spy notices posted in the town, and that riflemen guarded the men while engaged in the above operations.[101] It is difficult to understand how this level of republican activity could have been successfully carried out, in view of the numbers of Free State troops stationed in the town around that time. Republican intelligence officer, Andy O'Donoghue, reported that on 4

November, '200 cyclist troops entered Mallow' and on 5 November, he specified the buildings in which the Free State troops were stationed: 'Enemy forces in Mallow occupy the old barracks and the Presbyterian Church at the West End, Moran's private hotel, Thompson's Cycle shop, Thompson's Garage and Golden's Bridge Street.' He details the numbers of troops in each location and their armaments: 'Golden's 18 men 1 L gun, Moran's 25–30 men 1T Gun, 1 L gun.'[102] This intelligence shows that the garrison of Free State forces in Mallow around that time averaged 120 fully armed men, 'with the armoured car Dublin Liz in the garage'.[103] So during October, the Mallow battalion of Cork No. 4 brigade was doing much better than 'keeping pretty well together', had more than 'a little interest in the war' and the companies of the battalion were operating with impunity at parish level.

4

Difficulties for Republicans

COMMUNITY ALIENATION

Up to the end of October 1922, Liam Lynch's stated objective of not allowing the Provisional Government's writ to run was close to being achieved by the republicans of Cork No. 4 brigade in the rural areas of North Cork. Neeson advances some explanations for republican dominance in areas like North Cork: 'Although the towns were in the hands of the pro-Treatyites it became difficult for their troops to move outside without being ambushed.'[1] Neeson also argues that to defeat the guerrillas, 'they had to be cut off from towns where they might find succour'. Barring republicans from towns meant that the towns 'had to be garrisoned, immobilising large bodies of troops'.[2] This meant that the pro-Treaty troops were more or less confined to the towns, giving free rein to republicans in the countryside. Republican destruction of infrastructure surrounding towns – such as Charleville and Mallow – must also have severely limited the movement of Free State troops and reduced their capacity to restrict the actions of republicans around those towns. The republican leadership believed that the destruction of infrastructure and a systematic and continuous campaign of ambushes directed against the supply lines and communications of the pro-Treaty forces would give them the upper hand in the struggle.

However, Younger argues that these sustained guerrilla actions of ambush and destruction, did not actually indicate control and that at this stage of the Civil War, the National Army was winning the war by capturing and holding towns. As a result, 'it was obvious that the republicans could not win'.[3] Neeson agrees, saying that holding the towns meant that the Provisional Government had 'control of the country at large'. Therefore, in the context of the country as a whole, the limited success of guerrilla tactics 'seems to have blinded anti-Treaty commanders to the fact that they were merely local actions'.[4] While these tactics certainly restricted pro-Treaty military activity, they could not in themselves win the war.

The republicans' lack of awareness that destruction of infra-structure seriously discommoded rural communities in carrying out their daily activities affected their support in those same communities. Apart from shopping for the necessities of life, people wished to attend Sunday worship, children had to travel to school, it was necessary to transport milk to creameries and cattle had to be driven to fairs. In North Cork, it is no wonder that in many areas civilians were removing trees placed as barricades by the republicans to make a clear passage for their own travel. Not surprisingly, those in need were also taking some of these trees to use for firewood.[5] Republicans from Cork No. 4 brigade were incensed at civilian removal of barricades: 'it is not for fun or for firewood that trees are felled by our troops', they railed. It was decided that 'a notice will be put up on the barricade warning persons that if a barricade is interfered with a suitable punishment will be inflicted by our forces'. They went as far as to recommend 'that a bomb with the pin out should be placed in a stone barricade or where trees are laid'. For republicans, the maintenance of barricades to obstruct pro-Treaty troops superseded the value of human life, since they were satisfied that 'when the enemy or persons wanting to remove them try to do so well they will get the worst of it'.[6] This attitude appalled the affected communities. Neeson states that republican destruction of infrastructure, the barricading of roads and particularly attacks on the railways, served to further turn the anger of the general public against them.[7] Younger says that it seemed to many that 'for the sake of their ideals the republicans seemed bent on creating a pauperised people in a charred land'.[8]

Communication difficulties may have blinded republicans to the consequences of local guerrilla actions for local communities or for the country as a whole. Communication between anti-Treaty units was by means of verbal or written dispatches, carried on foot in many cases. As a result, reports were 'rarely received on a monthly, let alone a daily basis, as Lynch had required'. It was inevitable that republican GHQ was often ignorant of what was happening in the localities and was thus unable to influence local war efforts. General orders issued by GHQ 'counted for little when related to harsh local circumstances' and, extraordinarily, 'it seems the location of GHQ itself was unknown to most republicans'.[9] Paddy O'Brien, commandant of Cork No. 4 brigade, commented: 'When a general order was given … one area carried it out and the other didn't.'[10] Poor brigade communication with GHQ and also between local battalions led to uneven implementation of republican command orders and consequent confusion regarding republican policy in adjacent communities.

Losing the goodwill of the people can be disastrous for those engaged in a guerrilla campaign against superior forces well ensconced in towns. Neeson explains: 'the life of a guerrilla is hard; in winter almost insupportable. He is driven sooner or later, to seek refuge in farmhouses, in villages or in towns, where his security depends entirely on the support of the local inhabitants.'[11] He outlines three cardinal points necessary for a guerrilla: firstly, 'popular support' – the republicans' actions had angered many and eroded what support they had among neutrals; secondly, 'local knowledge' – this, republicans had in abundance; thirdly, 'goodly supplies' – by November, the inaccessibility of towns meant that adequate supplies were becoming scarcer.[12] For all the guerrillas, including the Cork No. 4 brigade under Commandant Paddy O'Brien, their position was becoming gruelling as the winter of 1922 set in.

Republican difficulties were further exacerbated when pro-Treaty forces began to move out of the towns in greater numbers and to intensify searches. The *Cork Examiner* of 1 November reports a successful raid on Mourneabbey and Rathduff by 'a column of fifty men of the National Troops from Mallow'. They arrested four Irregulars. The same paper reported five round-ups in the week ending Saturday 4 November in areas from Kanturk to Kiskeam and on to Rockchapel. In Kiskeam, they surrounded the church and searched 'all the male portion of the congregation on leaving'. They also discovered a well-supplied dugout.[13] On the same weekend, 'troops operating from Charleville arrested six active Irregulars' in the area, and on Tuesday 7 November they 'surrounded Lismire Hall, while a dance was in progress and made seven arrests, including Captain Tom Coughlan of Charleville'.[14] Tom Coughlan was an active republican and a serious loss to the Charleville battalion. In the same week, while these raids were in progress, republicans seized 'thirteen horses and cars from farmers in Milltown', near Charleville, and stole 'two overcoats from the residence of Mr Claude Keane, Milltown Castle'.[15] The loss of the coats did not trouble the Keane family unduly, but the commandeering of thirteen horses and cars seriously affected the capacity to travel of thirteen farming families.

THE SHOOTING OF MOLLY EGAN

The people of the village of Newtown were incensed when a local girl was shot during a round-up in the village by pro-Treaty forces. Michael Shine of Newtown was in the village on the night that Molly Egan was shot and he wrote the following account:

> In November 1922 the Civil War was raging between the Free Staters and the republicans. It was the evening of the Fair day in Charleville, a cold and dirty night and at that time

there were no lights in the village of Newtown, only whatever light shone from windows in the village.

Word came to Shine's in Newtown that the Staters in Charleville were to raid that night and if any of the republicans, the Boys as they were called, were there to warn them to get out of the village. In the pubs there was a share of them drinking. Some of them heeded the warning with the exception of Edmond McCarthy and Thomas Creagh. It was the case with them 'to let them all come'.

After a lot of persuasion they left in a pony and trap belonging to Hannigan's of Milford. As they came up the village they were giving a drive to Nora Fitzgerald, a maid at Mortell's, where Seán Flynn now lives, and Molly Egan also got a drive to the old school, as she was working at Denis Keane's, now Bobby Cotter's.

Molly remained in the trap and when she was coming back [sic] she should have got out at the old school and gone to her place of employment as she had a loaf of bread for Keane's.

The military were at the priest's big gate and as the trap was coming down the hill they opened fire into them and never cried 'halt!' They shot the pony in the legs and Molly being in front stood up and she was shot through the throat and died instantly.

McCarthy jumped over the priest's ditch and left his rifle after him [behind him] but he had a Peter the Painter revolver and was able to fire back. Creagh got away over Fleming's ditch and Hugh Aherne, a young gorsoon who was also in the trap, rolled down the road and got safely away into Drew's house. The Staters were firing at random all over the village because they were jittery and had no proper training. The officer in charge that night was a Captain Hannan and he was shaky too.

They took the pony from the trap. They wheeled it down to the cross and took Molly into Paddy Sullivan's. Father Blake, the parish priest, was brought down to give her the last rites and he anointed her in the room below the kitchen. My mother heard Father Blake's voice as he was passing the house. She knew someone was shot and she and my sister Lil followed Father Blake down to Sullivan's. They found poor Molly there and they washed her and laid her out.

In the meantime McCarthy came down inside the ditch opposite our house. I heard the whistle from inside the ditch so I went over and told him that Molly Egan was shot. He came into our house and stood with the revolver trained at the front door.

God help any Stater if he came to the front door. He would be gone with Molly Egan.[16]

The *Cork Examiner* of Tuesday 21 November, 1922 gave a comprehensive account of the inquest into the death of Molly Egan. In this account Captain James Hannan of the National Army stated that on Monday 13 November, he was in command of a party of forty men that went to make searches in the Newtownshandrum district. An outpost of three men was sent in the direction of the schoolhouse, while others searched the public houses in the village and captured two men – one man was armed and another was wearing a Sam Brown belt. Captain Hannan noted that he heard shooting in the direction of the schoolhouse and proceeded alone in that direction. When reinforcements arrived from the village, they approached the source of the sound, which they found was a horse and trap, and that the horse had been shot in the leg. Hannan ordered the trap to be searched and a service rifle and ammunition was found. He said that he found the deceased lying across the trap dead, and that they brought the body to Patrick O'Sullivan's and sent for the priest.

It is true that two republicans were in the trap and escaped, but two civilians were also in the trap. It is also true that shots were fired, but it is not certain who fired those fatal shots and when they were fired. What disturbed the people of the village was that shots were fired indiscriminately into a trap on the night in question with absolutely no regard for the lives of those occupying the trap.

The people were also incensed that the jury could not ascertain from the Free State forces who exactly fired the fatal shots.

The contradictions in the evidence of the Free State forces were not raised with Captain Hannan by Mr Binchy, solicitor for the Egans, or by the coroner. Hannan stated that on approaching the trap he had called out to his men and had been fired on. He took cover and called out again, and this time his men replied, saying that they were being fired on from the trap. Hannan called for the occupant to surrender and then fired about six shots at the trap. However, Private Breen of the outpost party stated that there had been no communication with Hannan until they had converged on the trap and that he never mentioned anyone firing from it. It may be that the captain was trying to cover up the possibility that his men had fired indiscriminately at the trap and killed an innocent girl. However, it may also be that when Captain Hannan, called to his men, they may have fired two shots in his direction in the mistaken belief that he was a republican. Those shots could not have killed Molly Egan because Captain Hannan said that he heard the bullets striking the road. However, when Captain Hannan fired his 'five or six shots in the direction of the car', it is possible that he not only shot the horse, but also the unfortunate Molly Egan. Hence his inaccurate evidence contradicted by his men.[17]

The jury retired and on return the foreman read the following verdict: 'That Molly Egan met her death by gunshot wounds, fired by the National Forces at Newtownshandrum, on the night of Monday the 13th of November.'[18] The verdict completely failed to address the controversy as to who exactly within the Free State forces was responsible for the reckless shooting of Molly Egan.

In the prevailing atmosphere of 1922, exemplified in New-townshandrum on 13 November, the conclusion of the foreman of the jury was untenable. He hoped that:

Irishmen would see eye to eye and end the terrible state of affairs in which they were living. The gun and the prison had failed to compose differences during the past 750 years and he hoped that Irishmen would come together now and settle their differences in an amicable manner.[19]

ESCALATION OF PRO-TREATY ACTIVITIES

The pro-Treaty forces continued to force the pace of round-ups relentlessly. In the week ending Thursday 16 November, nine round-ups were carried out by Mallow troops in areas from Killavullen to Kanturk, including two searches of Mourneabbey during the night.[20] The arrests apparently included those involved in 'the blowing up of bridges, highway and railway, including the Ten Arch Bridge' in Mallow.[21] Success was moderate in that arrests amounted to only ten or so, but as a result of the searches, republicans were feeling the pressure.

In the weekly summary of IRA activities dated 9 November 1922, the Charleville battalion of Cork No. 4 brigade – which had been very active in the autumn – reported that one company felled two trees. There was no report from any other company, and the other battalion companies received no mention at all. Two reports of sniping were recorded, but, most tellingly, the report concluded: 'no other activity owing to military [FS] being very active. Rounding up here.'[22] On 17 November the Mallow battalion, which had also been very active, reported seven snipings in its weekly summary. Mourneabbey was sniped at five times, one bridge had been destroyed and the rail line had been broken in one place. Two pro-Treaty raids were reported: one on Ballyclough and one on Fiddane. Seven arrests – including that of T. Ducey, O/C of C Company, and the battalion adjutant – were made at safe houses.[23] This level of activity was low by Mallow battalion standards and the capture of two senior officers was a blow to battalion morale. An extensive sweep of the Freemount and Tullylease areas was also made on 17 November. Pro-Treaty troops 'operating from Charleville, Kanturk and Newcastle West' cooperated in the sweep. They 'rounded up twenty active Irregulars', one of whom was 'a cousin of Seán Moylan, the well-known Irregular leader'.[24] These arrests are corroborated in an intelligence report by Andy O'Sullivan of Mallow: 'The capture of W. Moylan included one T gun, one L gun. Twenty arrests altogether around Tullylease and Freemount.'[25] Carrying out a triangular sweep of an area, using troops based in towns twenty kilometres apart, implies detailed, coordinated planning executed by well-trained pro-Treaty officers.

Pro-Treaty forces were also using small mobile flying columns to raid specific areas. On Tuesday 28 November, one of these columns of fifteen men 'proceeded from Charleville to the village of Dromina', where they 'rounded up' nine republicans.[26] In some of these round-ups, republican resistance was reported, and on a few occasions the pro-Treaty troops were ambushed. However, in most of the *Cork Examiner* reports no mention is made of any resistance or effort to evade arrest. Pro-Treaty persistence and deteriorating weather conditions were taking their toll on the republican guerrillas. Many republicans were being arrested in so-called safe houses in towns and villages. Andy O'Sullivan reported that prominent Mallow republicans Jackie Bolster, Cunningham, Morgan and Morrissey were arrested at 'trusted Kirkpatricks'.[27] The pro-Treaty policy of continuous harassment of republicans in their haunts and strongholds was beginning to have a telling effect on numbers and morale.

PROVISIONAL GOVERNMENT SPECIAL POWERS

On 27 September the Provisional Government took 'a courageous and conscience-searing decision' that had deadly implications for republicans and 'one which brought new horror into what was already a situation of tragic and growing bitterness'.[28] The Dáil gave the army special powers:

> … to hold military courts and to inflict severe penalties, including death, on men convicted of possession 'without proper authority' of firearms, ammunition or explosives; of arson looting or the destruction of private or public property; of taking part in, or aiding or abetting, attacks on the national forces; or of the breach of any general order or regulation made by the army council.[29]

On 10 October this granting of special emergency powers to the army was announced, and the powers were to take effect from 15 October. An amnesty was offered to republicans; it was open until 15 October provided they handed in their arms and took no further part in the Civil War. The full power and panoply of the Catholic Church was also ranged against republicans. Excommunication and exclusion from absolution and the Last Sacraments was the lot of any republican who fell in action or who was captured and executed.[30] The stance of the Catholic Church weighed heavily on devout republicans, but strangely, the special emergency powers, with their deadly implications, seemed not to have been taken seriously until the first executions took place on 17 November 1922, following the capture of four young men in Dublin 'with loaded guns in their possession and [who] were apparently preparing a street ambush'.[31]

Andy O'Sullivan gives the reaction in Mallow: 'The PG has started cold-blooded suppression in earnest, four young boys "shot at dawn."' He tells the story of the execution: 'A "Comdt" Doran ordered the shooting of the Mountjoy prisoners. The guards refused. "Vice Brig." Leonard lectured the mutineers, issued the orders again and there was another refusal. They were disarmed and arrested, 54 [in total], many of whom are in Mallow.'[32] This story cannot be corroborated, but if true indicates the revulsion of pro-Treaty soldiers regarding such executions, even among the Dublin Guards. On 10 November Erskine Childers was arrested at the family home of his cousin, Robert Barton, in Annamoe, County Wicklow.[33] He was captured with a small automatic pistol on his person that had been given to him by Michael Collins. Andy O'Sullivan again gives the reaction in Mallow: 'Childers is in a fight for his life. There were loud expressions of dissent even in FS circles.'[34] Nonetheless, Childers was executed on 24 November, dying 'with grace and heroism'.[35]

Republican CIC Liam Lynch 'was shocked and amazed at this execution policy'. On 27 November, he sent a letter to the speaker of the Provisional Parliament of Southern Ireland, in which he said:

> The illegal body over which you preside has declared war on the soldiers of the Republic … we on our side have at all times adhered to the recognised rules of warfare … you now presume to murder … the soldiers who had brought Ireland victory … we, therefore, give you and each member of your body, due notice that unless your army recognises the rules of warfare in the future, we shall adopt very drastic measures to protect our forces.[36]

Lynch followed this up with detailed instructions to commanding officers of all brigades, which could have left no doubt as to their intent. In an order dated 30 November 1922, he said:

> All members of Provisional Parliament who were present and voted for Murder Bill will be shot at sight. Attached find list of names. Houses of members of Murder Bill, Murder Gang and active supporters of PG who are known to support Murder Bill decision will be destroyed. All Free State army officers who approve of Murder Bill and are aggressive and active against our forces will be shot at sight;

also ex-British army officers and men who joined the Free State army since the 6th of December 1921. Individual action on paragraph 2/3 will be ordered by brigade O/C chief-of-staff.[37]

These orders were reiterated at local level. On 4 December 1922 the following letter was delivered 'To Commandant General Denis Galvin, Free State forces, Kanturk':

> At a meeting of the above brigade held on the 2nd inst. the following resolution was passed: 'That in the event of any man of Cork No. 4 brigade, Irish Republican Army, being executed; and that you countenance the carrying out of such orders by members of His Majesties Imperial Forces (of which you are one) that you would meet with the same fate, PEACE OR NO PEACE even though it may incur the loss of lives.'
>
> Further –
>
> 'That in the event of any man of Cork No. 4 brigade, Irish Republican Army, being executed, that an area of twelve miles be declared and that ten Free Staters be executed in that area for every one of our men executed.'
>
> Signed The officers and men of Cork No. 4 brigade IRA.[38]

Lynch's detailed instructions were distilled for the following letter from 'HQ 5th batt. Cork No. 4', and was addressed to 'The Chairman and members of Mallow Urban Council':

> From various sources it has come to my knowledge that the so-called Free State government – that traitorous junta of job hunters and slaves – are still determined to pursue their barbarous policy of murdering prisoners of the Republican Army. The ministers of that assembly say that it is the will of the people. Is it your will to execute men who have worked untiringly day and night in your service ... days without food and nights without shelter ... constant and faithful ...

remained incorruptible when many became corrupt? I think I have made it plain what view our forces have taken of your conduct in tolerating the murder policy of the FS. We hope the necessity for counter-reprisal will not arise in this area, but if it does then for every member from this area executed by the FS two members of the Mallow Advisory Committee will be shot as a reprisal. And next in order selections will be made from well-known and prominent FS supporters and sympathisers. Signed: Commdt.[39]

Hopkinson says that 'Liam Lynch had reservations about the implications of his own orders', and that he was conscious that 'reprisal killings would produce more executions and prove a death sentence for many republican prisoners'.[40] However, military orders from the commander-in-chief had to be followed, and republican brigade and battalion officers in North Cork took them absolutely seriously.

Others also took the reprisal orders seriously. On 7 December members of Dublin No. 1 brigade killed Brigadier Seán Hales and wounded Pádraic O'Maille, the Leas Cheann Comhairle of the Dáil, outside Leinster House.[41] At dawn the following morning, one prisoner from each of the four provinces – Liam Mellows, Rory O'Connor, Joseph McKelvey and Richard Barrett – were summarily executed without trial as a reprisal for the assassination of Seán Hales and also 'as a solemn warning to those who are associated with them who are engaged in a conspiracy of assassination against the representatives of the Irish people'.[42] The heart-rending last letter of Richard Barrett, from Cork, is testimony to the type of man he was. His last thoughts, having 'been called from his bed at 2 a.m.' to hear a paper being read that stated he was 'to be executed this morning at 8 a.m. as a reprisal for the murder of Seán Hales',[43] were for his family and his country:

For me the best has come, but for you all, I can picture you when you receive this news. I wish you would take it as cool and as resigned as I have done. Well I was not as good a son or brother as I might have been. I have caused you a lot of worry or uneasiness, but I know you will forgive me ... I should love to see you all, but this is impossible. I hope that we shall meet in Heaven, surely it will only be a few years at most. Mikey and Lizzey, and Jerry, Ciss, Mike, Robert and Dan will be sad, but little Jerry Collins and little Eileen Galvin when they grow up will glory in the triumphant cause of Irish freedom and will love to learn that I did not die for any other freedom than that for which Tone, Emmet and Pearse died.[44]

Dick Barrett's natural dignity, selflessness and his conviction that 'it is sweet and glorious to die for one's country' contrasts sharply with the bitterness and savagery of the closing phases of the Civil War.

On 6 December, 'at the height of the storm over the executions, the act establishing the Irish Free State completed its passage in the House of Commons'.[45] In an editorial, the *Cork Examiner* hailed the 'inauguration of the new Dominion of Ireland' as 'The Birth of Freedom'.[46] But the muted celebrations were irrelevant to the men on opposite sides in the field. Free State round-ups continued, and the 'Murder Bill' meant that the lives of republicans were forfeit if they were caught in possession of arms. 'Prominent Irregulars' were netted in a sweep of Milford and Dromina districts on Thursday 7 December, including brothers Con and Ned McCarthy of Newtown.[47] On Monday 11 December 'troops from Buttevant searched the Churchtown area' and surprised Peter O'Farrell and a number of other republicans who had been staying 'at Winters for two days'.[48] O'Farrell recalls hiding 'their rifles in the fox cover two fields away', and being 'given the works about the guns by a Free State officer'.[49] On Thursday 14 December, Free State troops were ambushed during a round-up near Millstreet, and the *Cork*

Examiner reports that some days later, four Irregulars – including two captains and a brigadier – were captured 'at Drishanebeg near Millstreet'.[50] There was no respite during the Christmas season. On Christmas Eve, 'Newtownshandrum, Dromina and Liscarroll districts were raided leading to the capture of three Irregulars', and on Christmas Day, 'troops from Charleville, while carrying out searches in the Milford area, arrested two well-known Irregulars, Drum and Crowley'. Only three minor republican incidents were reported during the week prior to Christmas.[51]

MILLSTREET AND AUGHRIM

The new year began on a relatively quiet note. Round-ups were carried out in Churchtown on 2 January and in Newtown on 3 January. However, the *Cork Examiner* of 6 January reported that fire was opened on 'a party of National Troops' close to Newmarket, and that the 'Irregulars were under the command of T. Barry, a well-known member of the Irregular forces'. The presence of Tom Barry in the locality should have alerted the Free State authorities to an imminent attack. That attack came in Millstreet on Thursday 4 January 1923. It was described by the *Cork Examiner* as 'a desperate and carefully planned attack' made on 'the military posts in Millstreet'.[52] The seriousness of the attack warranted a special investigation by Commandant General Galvin, O/C 1st Southern Division of the Free State forces. He reported from HQ 1st Southern Division, Kanturk, on 8 January 1923 as follows:

> Re the attack on Millstreet. I have the honour to report that I visited Millstreet on Sunday Jan. 7th '23 for the purpose of fully investigating the attack by Irregulars on that town. The strength of the attacking party was at least 300 not counting the number they used to hold the different roads and approaches to the town. The main body of the Irregulars came from the Kerry border, a large proportion from Ballyvourney.

They were assisted by local Irregulars from Millstreet and a party from North Cork. L. Lynch and T. Barry were the two principal leaders in the attack. The first object of the attack was to destroy the wireless station, which was erected at the end of the town, 300 yards from the HQ at the Carnegie Hall. This post was taken completely by surprise and captured, the sentry being shot by Thompson gunfire, receiving ten bullet wounds. Two other posts were simultaneously surprised and captured, Murphy's in the centre of the town and a post known as the old police barracks. This post made a gallant stand for at least three hours until finally, their ammunition being exhausted and as the Irregulars were pouring Thompson gun fire and rifle grenades into their position, they were compelled to surrender. In these three posts the Irregulars captured one Lewis gun and thirty-five rifles. The next attack was launched on HQ at the end of the town, known as the Carnegie Hall. On this post the most determined attack was made. The Irregulars used six machine-guns and concentrated a heavy fire on the building from various vantage points. Our troops, who numbered twenty-three, had only one Lewis gun in the building and replied vigorously to the fire of the attackers who advanced under cover of machine-gun fire as far as the entrance of the hall and succeeded in setting fire to the door. Were it not for the bravery of Sgt Maj. J. O'Mahony, who rushed in the face of machine-gun fire and succeeded in quenching the fire, the whole building would have been burned to the ground. It was whilst engaged in putting out the fire that this gallant W.O. was killed, leaving the army to mourn the loss of a very brave soldier. He leaves a widow and three children. Great credit is also due to the bravery of the Lewis gunner, Vol. John Kelleher, who did not wait even to dress, but rushed to his post and poured a continuous fire on the Irregular position. The following are also worthy of recommendation. Capt. H. Kiely, O/C of the town, Lieut Bissett, Vol. James O'Sullivan and Vol. Bohan. These men were mainly instrumental in saving the town and it was due in great extent to their efforts that the Irregulars were forced to withdraw. The main body of the Irregulars, who are supposed to have suffered heavy casualties, six at least being killed, retreated in the direction of the two Pap Mountains in Kerry and the remainder in the direction of Ballyvourney. The morale of our troops in Millstreet is very high and every man considers the withdrawal of the Irregulars a victory for the National Army. The men are held in very high esteem by the civilian population of the town and they are very loud in their praise for their gallant defence of the town against overwhelming odds. The houses of Capt. Kiely and Lieut Tagney, both natives of Millstreet, were looted by the Irregulars before their departure and a considerable quantity of clothing was taken, including millinery. It has been ascertained that of the two who attacked and shot the sentry at the wireless station, one was dressed as a priest and the other as a woman.[53]

This account is corroborated in the *Cork Examiner* of 8 January with some minor differences. The *Cork Examiner* says that 'the Irregular in clerical dress is supposed to have been Liam Lynch. It was he who shot the sentries.' The republican casualties are reported by the doctor in attendance as seven killed and nineteen wounded, and 'the Post Office was also visited and all money taken'.[54] The republican attitude to the attack is summarised in a letter from the O/C 1st Southern Division to O/C all commands. 'The Millstreet stunt was damned good. The fire was a terror – twelve M[achine] guns. Sixty-five of our fellows were there, they captured thirty-nine prisoners, thirty-eight rifles and one Lewis gun. Such a night never fell out of the heavens. Two of ours slightly wounded and one badly.'[55] Despite the note of glee in the report, not capturing the town was a serious setback for a republican column said to have been led by CIC Liam Lynch and Tom Barry, and a commensurate blow to their morale. Pro-Treaty relief at the successful defence of the town must have been tempered by the knowledge that, despite many republican casualties, many prisoners had been taken by the republicans and that the pro-Treaty forces had not dented the capacity of the republicans to mount serious attacks on well-garrisoned towns.

The size of the republican column that attacked Millstreet is unclear – accounts vary from 300 in Commandant Galvin's report to sixty-five in the republican report. The *Cork Examiner*, put the number at 'close on 150 with 18 machine-guns'.[56] This column then seems to have billeted around Freemount and Dromina because, on Wednesday 17 January, 'troops from Charleville, under Comdt Cronin and Comdt O'Brien, encountered a large party of Irregulars, near Dromina on the Freemount side', while engaged in rounding-up operations. They arrested four armed republicans. However, when the troops 'proceeded in the direction of Freemount', they were attacked 'by about a hundred Irregulars who used Thompson guns, rifles and Peter the Painters'.[57] This engagement seems to have petered out before a second engagement took place, beginning at Aughrim Cross:

> Comdt Cronin's section was engaged by another Irregular outpost in the direction of Freemount. The entire column was beaten back across country in the direction of Freemount … and a pitched battle ensued for over three hours. Our troops held the position they had gained … awaiting reinforcements from Buttevant. As these were delayed … our troops were obliged to retreat in the Liscarroll direction. Here they were joined by the column from Buttevant. Both columns then returned to the place of attack … the Irregulars were greatly reinforced and had a column of 150 men … our troops were greatly outnumbered being only 50 strong. Irregulars were under the command of Alph. Conroy and Paddy O'Brien.[58]

The Free State troops were forced to disengage and retire to base.

The Aughrim battle and the Millstreet attack indicated a revitalised republican campaign, with much larger numbers in combined columns. The republicans came within a whisker of capturing Millstreet and they had the better of the Free State troops in the Aughrim encounter. A change to operating in large columns seemed to enhance their prospects of success. In mid-January their star seemed to be in the ascendant again in North Cork.

5

The Free State Takes Control

DETERIORATION IN REPUBLICAN MORALE

The intensification of republican activity in North Cork by Cork No. 4 brigade in early January did not reflect the republican position throughout the country. Hopkinson sums up the situation: 'The first four months of 1923 saw a progressive disintegration of the republican military effort.' He quotes a Cork republican writing to Pa Murray:

> The Staters have all areas overan [*sic*] and if a column start off the next you find is a few thousand of the enemy rounding up. Columns cannot exist except in small parties and jobs are few and far between the rule of the torch and can are proved to be more effective ... Making Government impossible is your only chance of success ...[1]

In general, republicans were becoming demoralised. Their overall military position was bleak, their war materials and essential supplies were steadily diminishing and, to avoid capture, many had to take refuge high in the hills and in well-concealed dugouts. Neeson confirms this:

> By spring 1923 the anti-Treatyites were in a bad way. Their position was hopeless ... Columns still in the field were being harassed without rest by superior forces. The 'Republican Itch' and general fatigue were rampant, supplies were scarce, and clothing and equipment were unobtainable. The end was inevitable ...[2]

O'Donoghue says that 'the Free State Government was imbued powerfully ... by the will to win the struggle no matter how ruthless the means', whilst, in contrast, the republican forces as a whole 'had lost that essential moral constituent of success'. For Catholic republicans and their families, the fact that 'the Church had outlawed them' was devastating, and, crucially for guerrillas, 'the people, except a minority, regarded their fate with indifference'.[3]

The general public, and especially the diminishing republican community, could not have been indifferent to the escalation of executions in early 1923. Florence O'Donoghue states that: 'By the end of January, 1923, fifty-five executions had been carried out; many others were pending',[4] although Hopkinson puts the number of executions at thirty-four.[5] However, Younger argues that the people had in fact become hardened to this system of executions, and that, rather than causing outrage, 'in a curious way [they] respected the government for its determination to win complete control at any cost'.[6] Hopkinson disagrees and suggests that it is extremely unlikely that friends and relatives of republicans were not 'heavily influenced' by the executions.[7]

In early 1923 the Free State government introduced a new policy 'of suspending death sentences, on condition that hostilities ended in the localities of the sentenced men'.[8] This imposed considerable strain on the men in the prisons and 'a more terrible responsibility on their comrades who were fighting outside'.[9] Inevitably, greatly increased pressure to suspend or conclude hostilities was brought to bear on republican guerrillas, their supporters and their families, by the families, friends and relatives of those in prison under a sentence of death. As mentioned above, republican Liam Moylan of Newmarket was captured in possession of arms in November 1922. On 26 February 1923 Andy O'Sullivan of Mallow reported that Moylan was in the 'condemned cells in Limerick' along with Cunningham, Bolster and Morgan of Mallow, who had been arrested on 15 November 1922. O'Sullivan reported that Liam

Moylan's brother, Con Moylan, 'O/C transport' of the Newmarket battalion, 'surrendered in Newmarket and returned to induce all members of the Newmarket battalion, now in the column, to surrender before Sunday night as a means of saving his brother Liam', who 'is supposed to have been told that execution is fixed for Monday morning unless his pals surrender'.[10] The threat of Liam's execution put Con Moylan under intolerable pressure. His brother's life was at stake and he buckled under the strain. His surrender and subsequent request placed his fellow republicans in the column in a terrible dilemma.

Newmarket republicans were not the only ones under pressure to desist. When Cunningham, Bolster and Morgan were being taken to Limerick jail in November 1922, their supporters turned out in large numbers. Their vociferous and aggressive support for the three men caused their guards to 'get windy at the size of the crowd' as they 'cheered for Dev and the Republic, until fire was opened up by the prisoners' escort'.[11] Bolster had many connections in Mallow and had been a key member of the Volunteers who took part in the celebrated raid on Mallow barracks on 28 September 1920 during the War of Independence. In February 1923 the people of Mallow were reminded, in a republican bulletin, that 'this policy of executions is being carried out in the name of the Irish people ... the people of Mallow are requested to take immediate and active steps to show the FS Govt that it is not their will to execute prisoners of war'.[12]

The Mallow people rallied behind Bolster and mounting public opinion caused Mallow Urban Council to call 'a specially convened meeting' on 19 February. At this meeting, it was decided unanimously to send a wire to President Cosgrave and General Mulcahy urgently requesting them 'to postpone the execution of these men as there are facts relating to their cases which we believe would be sufficient to obtain for them a reprieve'. To support the request, 'a petition from the people of Mallow, influentially signed, will be forwarded in due course'.[13] It is unlikely that this petition was initiated as a result of the republican threat made to Mallow Urban Council following Liam Lynch's reprisal order of 30 November 1922. Mallow Urban Council was heavily pro-Treaty. It is more likely that the petition was drawn up because of the horror engendered among Mallow people by the threatened execution of three local men. This horror inevitably placed equivalent pressure on Mallow republicans to restrain themselves and their activities in the 5th battalion area.

THE DEASY DEBACLE

Liam Deasy was highly regarded by both republicans and Free Staters alike, but for different reasons. He was deputy chief-of-staff of the republican forces, 'a member of the executive and officer commanding Lynch's Southern Command'.[14] General Emmet Dalton, of the Free State army, told the chairman of Cork County Council that they wanted to get Deasy 'as he is the most resourceful officer in republican ranks and if they had him the end would be in sight. While he is at large the war will go on.'[15] Consequently, the capture of Liam Deasy on 18 January was a huge blow to the republican campaign.[16] De Valera said that his capture was 'the biggest blow … since we started'.[17]

Neeson describes Deasy as 'perhaps the most brilliant of the anti-Treaty officers; certainly none more sincere or devoted to the republican cause than he'.[18] Interestingly O'Donoghue says that, prior to capture, Deasy 'was already satisfied that the time had come when armed resistance should cease', and that 'other means should be found to realise the republican ideals'.[19] Hopkinson agrees, stating that 'Deasy had represented the most important example of the Cork IRA's reluctant participation in the conflict', and that Deasy later 'told colleagues that he had been preparing for peace negotiations and was planning to see Lynch about this'.[20]

There is no doubt that the capture of the GOC of the 1st Southern Division was a devastating blow to the republican cause. However, what happened next caused consternation in republican ranks.

Deasy was 'tried by court martial' on 25 January, found guilty of 'having in his possession, without proper authority, one long Parabellum revolver and twenty-one rounds of ammunition', and was duly sentenced to death.[21] Younger says that the firing squad was selected and at 4 a.m. on 26 January, 'Deasy was ready for death, calm and courageous'.[22] Neeson says 'there is no doubt that the sentence made no difference to Deasy, but he was more anxious than ever that the war should cease, now that it was no longer possible for him to place his views before the anti-Treaty executive'.[23] O'Donoghue states that Deasy's desire to end the conflict 'put him in a position of extraordinary difficulty and strain', and that his conviction 'of the imperative necessity for some action to terminate the conflict' led him to ask his captors for permission to contact his colleagues to achieve that aim.[24] A stay of execution was ordered and, following negotiations, Deasy signed a pro-Treaty document stating that he would aid in an immediate unconditional surrender of men and arms, and that he would appeal to Liam Lynch and the members of the republican executive to do likewise. He was allowed to send a covering letter with this document to his colleagues explaining his reasoning for his acceptance of the pro-Treaty document – he felt that it was time the war was ended, as he believed the hostilities were destroying the country.[25] This letter was published in the *Cork Examiner* of 10 February.

Initially, Liam Lynch believed that Deasy's letter had to be a forgery,[26] while Mallow republicans believed it was a 'stunt', and that 'the civil population here' were 'swallowing it grand'.[27] Seán Moylan wrote from the United States on 23 February, commenting: 'Deasy's attitude knocked me silly. I thought he'd be the last man to cave in.' However, he grudgingly conceded, 'it wasn't cowardice on his part, I know'.[28] Tom Barry, perhaps surprisingly given the republicans, lack of military success, claimed 'it was Deasy who put the Tin Hat on us … we were at our highest level of success … when the Deasy Manifesto crippled us'.[29] Yet, the same Tom Barry signed his name to peace moves published in the *Cork Examiner* on 8 March 1923.

The republican leadership tried to close ranks and Deasy's ideas for negotiating peace were rejected. On 10 February Tom Barry wrote from IRA Field General Headquarters to the O/Cs of all the divisions of Southern Command, saying:

> It will be fully explained to the men that on no account will any men or arms be surrendered to the enemy, also that no officers or men will be allowed to surrender to the enemy and arms in their possession. Such action will receive very drastic treatment.[30]

Paddy O'Brien, Commandant Cork No. 4 brigade, wrote to his officers stating:

> A unanimous answer was sent to the former DCS on behalf of the govt and the army by the chief-of-staff, refusing to even consider such proposals and re-iterating that the fight would go on until INDEPENDENCE was attained. Any man who surrenders will be dealt with drastically.

The communication also notified that 'a brigade meeting will be held in Freemount on Thursday night [15 Feb.] at 6 p.m.', and that 'D. Willis must attend'.[31] Willis was a Mallow battalion member who had also taken part in the raid on Mallow barracks on 28 September 1920. He would have been most anxious to save his fellow battalion member, Bolster, from execution. Although it is not specified in the communication what the meeting was for, it was probably an attempt to stem resignations from the Cork No. 4 brigade.

Despite the warnings contained in Barry and O'Brien's statements, some of the republican officers, as well as rank and file members, became disaffected. Hopkinson notes, 'Deasy's action did nothing to encourage men in the ranks to fight to the death', and quotes John Joe Rice commenting, 'it created an air of unreality, for we weren't sure which of the important officers would go next'.[32]

Deasy's actions and his appeal, coupled with the escalation of executions, had a dramatic effect on prisoners. One republican commented to Liam Lynch that: 'All the enemy do now is issue a *threat* of execution and the men will give way.'[33] Six hundred prisoners, through eleven nominated leaders, made an appeal to the GOC Limerick Command to request permission from 'your GHQ in Dublin to allow four men from this prison to get parole and proceed to our leaders outside to place before them' the view that 'the present struggle is a waste of blood and has developed into a war of extermination'. The prisoners believed 'it has gone far enough and ought to stop now'.[34] While it is unlikely that this appeal for peace by 600 prisoners was made under threat of imminent execution, republicans allege that 'the prison population … was ruthlessly used by the Free State to influence the situation outside'.[35] A letter, 'unsigned, as the receiver will be able to recognise the writer', was received by the Mallow battalion:

> The O/C was pulled out of bed at midnight and threatened with instant death if he did not write a letter similar to that of Deasy's. He refused always. There was no body of persons more surprised than the prisoners here when they heard in the paper that they were craving for peace … I think I would be voicing the majority of the prisoners feelings when I'd wish the war to be continued even for years or at least no surrendering of principles. One of the main arguments

[presented to] Seán Mac Lainchin, our O/C, was that the blood of every man executed would be upon him as he had the way of stopping them executing them.[36]

Internal Free State pressure or not, another appeal was made to General Prout, GOC Waterford Command, on 10 February 'on behalf of ninety-eight prisoners detained in Clonmel'.[37] Hopkinson outlines how 'six prisoners asked for parole [from Cork jail] … with a view to putting the full facts before their superior officers'. The parole was granted and at a meeting of the 1st Southern Division in late February, these men made it quite clear that 'no matter what orders they got from outside … [they] would sign Deasy's document, as it was preferable to being executed'.[38] Kerry prisoners in Tralee jail approved 'of Liam Deasy's action in calling on his comrades for unconditional surrender', and sent their appeal to the GOC Kerry. In little over a month, Tom Barry had converted to the cause of peace, and agreed on 4 March 1923 to circulate peace proposals received from 'T. O'Dubugain, Sagart … for immediate consideration amongst the members of the IRA Executive Council'.[39] Despite initial rejection, Deasy's views were beginning to take root.

Republicans in the field were also influenced by Deasy's actions, despite the dire warnings initially issued by Tom Barry. 'Twenty-seven young Irishmen … in County Westmeath' decided 'to take no further action in the campaign'. In North Cork, on 8 February, 'a number of Irregulars in the Kanturk district' surrendered their arms at Kanturk barracks, and on 10 February 'a number of Irregulars, including a captain' surrendered arms and ammunition at Newmarket military barracks.[40] In Kerry, 'an Irregular leader named Pierce, commanding two Irregular columns in north Kerry' decided 'to surrender all arms and men'.[41] He was referred to as 'Mr Michael Pierce' when he received the personal appreciation of President Cosgrave, who said: 'I appreciate most heartily the very honourable action of yourself and your men, taken, to use Deasy's words for the "future of Ireland".'[42]

To try to stem the tide of surrenders, HQ 1st Southern Division issued a chilling general order to the O/Cs of all units on 8 March: 'From the date of this order any Volunteer who surrenders himself or any area to the enemy will be tried by court martial on a charge of treason and if convicted will be shot.'[43] Notwithstanding these orders, the *Cork Examiner* reported that Liam Deasy's action 'together with the action of 600 men in Limerick prison was received in Killarney with the greatest satisfaction'. Also, 'a hopeful feeling' prevailed 'amongst the people of North Cork as to the possibilities of an early peace', since 'no fighting has taken place for the past two weeks'. Furthermore, the paper stated that 'the dramatic turn of events during the past week or two' and the prospect of peace 'will be hailed with relief and satisfaction by the people of North Cork who are sick of war and all its attendant evils'.[44]

RELENTLESS ROUND-UPS

The optimistic tenor of the *Cork Examiner* reports was tempered by the January monthly confidential report of the Civic Guard, the new Free State police force, for Cork East Riding. The report stated that 'the area continues unsatisfactory' and 'behind all this is the menacing aspect of the "political situation" or armed opposition to the Government'. The report summarised that this opposition was directly responsible for eighty per cent of crimes committed in the area, and while 'formerly chiefly directed against the army and army posts … it is now concentrated with a view to ruin on the economical side', with destruction of the 'railways and all sources of revenue for the state – Rent Annuities, Post Offices, Income Tax … [and] Dog Tax'.[45] Economic ruin could not be tolerated and it became imperative for the Free State government to eliminate armed activity in areas such as North Cork. Yet this still proved to be a difficult task, requiring the commitment of large numbers of troops based in the towns of the area, such as Charleville, as in mid-January a large column of republicans – 'strength ninety-three, one hundred rifles, ammunition plentiful' – led by Commandant Paddy O'Brien was operating in the area with substantial support in the hinterland.[46] This intensified republican activity is confirmed in another report of 21 January: 'Charleville Area. Large force of Irregulars have been operating in this area and traces of their activity are shown in the blocking of roads and railways. Shinana bridge came into the line of destruction.'[47]

The Free State Limerick Command, who commanded North Cork as well, responded by implementing highly organised sweeps of known republican haunts by large numbers of troops, and searches of smaller troublesome areas using mobile columns with reduced numbers of troops. The *Cork Examiner* reported that on 23 February 'while a party of troops were searching houses in Liscarroll, they were fired on from Egan's public house. The Irregulars, who were having tea at the time, got away at the backdoor under cover of darkness.' The Military Archive records of this raid provide a picture of a much more dramatic affair. A 'party under Capt. Guerin raided Liscarroll. Corporal O'Meara went into Egan's public house to enquire about O'Briens. Mrs Noonan, schoolmistress at Churchtown, rushed to the door of the dining room and shouted to some men to run.' In the mêlée, 'fire was opened on Corporal O'Meara and the men in the room made their escape' as 'Mrs Noonan was grappling with Corporal O'Meara'. Mrs Noonan, 'wife of Seán Noonan, Irregular' was subsequently arrested on 10 March.[48]

This unsuccessful raid provoked a sweep of the area on 26 February, planned by Commandant Cronin commanding the 39th Infantry battalion, Charleville. The following are the detailed plans for the sweep drawn up by Cronin:

Objective

- It is proposed to surround and search the village of Liscarroll at 8 a.m. on the morning of 26th Feb. 1923. A small column of Irregulars numbering from ten to twelve all armed with rifles, leader P. O'Brien, are reported to be in this area. All available men from Buttevant and Charleville posts will cooperate in this operation.

Task A

- Capt. Domican will leave Charleville with thirty men accompanied by Lt Dennehy at 2 a.m. and proceed to Newtown school. Here he will divide into two columns No. 1 and 2.
- Column 1 will proceed to search Corrough and intervening country to Dromina. The houses of Messrs Daly and Boyce of Corrough receiving special attention, after leaving Dromina they will continue to all houses adjacent to the Dromina–Liscarroll road, thoroughly searching the Sunfort district.
- Column 2 will search all houses in the Curraglas, Ballinala and Aughrim districts, special attention to the following houses: Flynn's of Prohurst, Dwane's Ballinala, Fitzgerald's Aughrun, O'Donnell's Aughrun and Barry's Aughrun.

Task B

- Comdt Cronin will also leave Charleville at 2 a.m., proceed to Miltown [*sic*] via upper road, search all houses adjacent to the road. All houses in the Ardglass district will be thoroughly searched. The following receiving special attention: Wallace's Ardglass. Flynn's do. Callaghan's do. Dan Cagney's Miltown. As well as all houses in front of Hoofers [*sic*], then on to Killabraher then on to Ardagh special attention to the houses of Regan's, Naughton's and Galvin's in the Ardagh area, then on to Altimira, thence to Liscarroll.

Task C

- Capt. Guerin will leave Buttevant with all available men at 2 a.m. on the morning of the 26th Feb. and proceed to Templemary, search all the country from Templemary into Liscarroll particularly around Ardprior, paying special attention to Noonan's and all houses in its vicinity.

- All columns will close on the village of Liscarroll at the appointed time and search it thoroughly.
- Reports of operations will be compiled and sent to batt. headquarters immediately on completion of operations.[49]

A Special Operations Report was sent to the Command Adjutant at the Field GHQ Limerick:

- On the morning of the 26th inst. Comdt Cronin, Capts Costello and Domican, Lieuts Dennehy and Kierse, with a column of sixty-six men left Charleville at 2 a.m. proceeded to Liscarroll and searched the following districts.
- Capt. Domican, with twenty men searched Corrough, and country into Dromina, paying special attention to Daly's and Boyces of Corrough, Lieut Kierse with twenty-three men searched all the houses in Curraglass, Ballinala and Aughrim; Flynn's Prohurst, Dwane's, Ballinala, Fitzgerald's, Barry's and O'Donnell's Aughrim, received special attention.
- Comdt Cronin, with sixteen men searched all houses in Miltown [sic], Ardglass, Kilabraher [sic], Ardagh, Altymira [sic], including Wallace's, Flynn's, Callaghan's Ardglass, Regan's Naughton's and Galvin's of Kilabraher.
- Capt. Guerin with forty-four men left Buttevant, at 2.30 a.m. on the 26th for Liscarroll, searched all houses, in Templemary and Ardaprior [sic] districts. Both the Charleville and Buttevant columns closed on Liscarroll village at 9 a.m. and searched it thoroughly for a column of armed Irregulars who were supposed to be in the village the previous day.
- On return journey to Buttevant Capt. Guerin's column searched the village at Churchtown and made four arrests all unarmed.[50]

The arrested men were listed in the report and two were released by Captain Guerin on signing the necessary undertaking.

A similar operation, but on a much larger scale, had been

undertaken on 3 February by General Liam Hayes of the Limerick Command. This sweep involved 'detachments from Charleville, Newcastle West, Abbeyfeale, Newmarket, Kanturk [and] Buttevant', with 'Freemount the objective'.[51] The files in the Military Archives record thirty-one such searches or sweeps in the area under the Free State Charleville Command between 23 January and 13 March 1923. This means that some areas were searched at least every second day. Two areas were recorded as being searched three times and four areas were searched twice in one day. As outlined above, the searches were meticulously planned: the Free State forces had detailed knowledge of the topography of the areas to be searched and of the regular billets used by republicans. In many cases, it would appear that they also had prior knowledge of the whereabouts of the republicans. The columns of Cork No. 4 brigade were being harried relentlessly and their existence was becoming more precarious by the day. Neeson concluded that well-planned and effectively executed pro-Treaty round-ups, together with diminishing support from the people, meant that it was 'only a matter of time before proper garrisons in the towns and proper mobile columns on the roads' would 'render the existence of guerrillas impossible'.[52]

Commandant Ned Cronin, commander of the 39th Free State Infantry Battalion, based in Charleville, waged a war of attrition on the republicans in the Charleville area. In an inspection of his command on 23 February, he is described as 'a keen, efficient officer' and 'from an operation [*sic*] point of view the battalion could not be working better'.[53] The total strength of Commandant Cronin's battalion was 320 men. The same report estimates that republican Commandant Paddy O'Brien had 'twenty-seven men, two T guns and twenty-seven rifles'. The report recounts that there were twenty-four operations undertaken by Cronin's battalion during that month. Paddy O'Brien and the republicans were being hounded from pillar to post, and they were outnumbered and out-gunned. Cronin kept the pressure up; in an inspection held on 26 April 1923, it is reported that he had commanded 'fifteen operations from 9.4.23 to 26.4.23' – practically one anti-republican operation per day. At that stage, his battalion strength was 426 men. It is no wonder that the report concluded: 'republican leaders, Paddy O'Brien, Seán Noonan, Seán O'Brien. Nil activity.'[54] Neeson sums up such round-ups graphically: 'The procedure was becoming like a fox hunt, with, in all too many cases, a like end to the chase and a consequent demoralisation', for both the hunted and, in some cases, the hunters.[55] The local republicans hated 'the Lion Tamer, Ned Cronin'. Peter O'Farrell and others had been arrested in December 1922. Despite the air of bravado in his account of the arrest, the fear and apprehension of the republican prisoners can be sensed in his description of Ned Cronin swaggering around the parochial hall in Charleville 'kicking their feet and delivering a snarling lecture!'[56] Local, uncorroborated sources claim that in the aftermath of the Civil War, Ned Cronin was subjected to republican revenge on a dark night, having left a pub in Milford to return to Charleville.

The table following summarises the position of Cork No. 4 brigade as reported in the Civil War operations files of the Free State Limerick Command.[57] The recorded leadership of the brigade varied slightly, but, in general, it was under the command of Paddy O'Brien. The membership fluctuated, possibly due to arrests, but apart from a high of ninety-three in January, the average membership was fifty-two. Their area of operations was relatively small, so the ability to support an active column of this size indicates that the republicans still had widespread community backing in this area. This may account for the lack of information received by the Free State forces in North Cork, as indicated under the heading 'Comment' in the table. The republicans were well armed and had motor transport up to the end of March. Their main activity was the destruction of infrastructure, with occasional sniping at Free State posts. The most telling report in the table is the collapse of republican morale in May.

Table 2: *General Weekly Returns, 1923*

Date	Leaders	Men	Rifles	T Guns	Lewis Guns	Ammunition
12 Jan. 1923	P. O'Brien J. O'Connor P. O'Donnell S. Noonan M. Sheehan	93	100	0	0	Plentiful
3 Feb. 1923	As Above	38	38	2	0	
10 Mar. 1923	As Above				0	
24 Mar. 1923	As Above	53	53	2	0	Plentiful
14 Apr. 1923	P. O'Brien E. McCarthy S. Noonan D. Motherway	60	60	3	0	Unknown
17 Apr. 1923	D. Breen P. Donavan E. Walsh				0	
25 Apr. 1923	As Above	54	50	2	0	Unknown
28 Apr. 1923	E. McCarthy D. Motherway	34	34	1	0	Unknown
12 May 1923	P. O'Brien, N. McCarthy C. McCarthy S. Noonan D. Motherway	47	51	2	1	Plentiful
17 May 1923	N. McCarthy C. McCarthy Shanahan	43	60	1	1	Unknown
24 May 1923	N. McCarthy C. McCarthy	43	70	1	1	Unknown
31 May 1923	N. McCarthy S. Noonan D. Motherway	45	50	1	1	Unknown

Motor Bikes	Lorries	Bicycles	Assessments by FS officers
0	0	0	Destruction of infrastructure.
1	0	0	None.
			Twelve arrested including Owen Egan, Liscarroll; Buckley, Freemount and Mrs Noonan, wife of Seán Noonan, Irregular.
3	4	Some	Activities slack. Whole-time [full-time] and local columns.
Unknown	0	0	Raiding POs. Trenching. Strength on the decrease. Information more freely.
			Arrested in dugout, Longford Aherlow.
Unknown	0	0	Reorganising. Small columns. Morale optimistic. Civilian population sympathetic. Little information. Hinder govt.
Unknown	0	0	Raiding PO Bruree. Decreasing in number. People unsympathetic. Commandeering cars.
	0	0	Strength on decrease. Small roving bands. No coop. between columns. Pop. still hostile. Info difficult.
Unknown	0	0	Irreg. inactive. Whole-time col. active. Local col. do destruction, v. active. People support govt. Morale of rank and file low. Desertions. Arms dumped.
Unknown	0	0	Morale very low. Civil pop. anti-Irreg. Information given more freely. No activity.
Unknown	0	0	Morale completely broken. Leaders and men not cooperating, scattering in small helpless parties. No activities. People more friendly to our troops.

The 5th battalion of Cork No. 4 brigade in Mallow, were also experiencing difficulties. On 31 December 1922, the arms held in the battalion area were 'rifles 30, revolvers 10, ammunition 800 rds of .303'. They were fighting against Free State forces with 112 rifles and seven machine-guns in Mallow, and an average of forty-eight men in each of the surrounding villages, such as Mourneabbey and Twopothouse. It is no wonder that the battalion weekly summary of activities dated 1 February 1923 included only 'four sniping activities and wires cut twice'. They did, however, raid six post offices in the area. This had been a very active and successful battalion – it had reported seven snipings, one major attack on Mourneabbey, two bridges destroyed and the rail line broken once in the weekly report ending 16 November 1922.[58] But the Mallow battalion had a torrid time in the spring of 1923. On 30 April a report indicated that the vice officer commanding position was vacant and that the quartermaster was inactive. While they had forty men on their roll, they had only three rifles, two revolvers and a total of fifty bullets. A devastating report, dated 1 May, recorded that the '5th batt. officers had been captured. Six O/Cs, five Lieut. one vice O/C and one I/O. Seven deserted or resigned'.[59]

By the end of May 1923, the two best battalions of Cork No. 4 brigade, Mallow and Charleville, were decimated. As in County Cork as a whole, at the end of the Civil War – as recalled by Mick Murphy – 'republicans resembled wandering sheep.'[60] Although there had never been an outright defeat of the republicans, the pro-Treaty forces had progressively worn down their will to continue the struggle.[61]

THE CIVIL WAR DRAWS TO A CLOSE

In keeping with the situation countrywide, a number of factors, when accumulated, hastened the end of the Civil War in North

Cork. The decision of the Free State side to execute prisoners, coupled with the Deasy affair, had rocked the republican side to its foundations. Moreover, the cumulative effect of peace moves by influential groups inevitably affected republican resolve and morale. The Free State army had the support of the majority of the population and the Catholic Church, as well as the backing of a government with substantial resources. The republicans only had a 'government' in name, grudgingly granted by Liam Lynch. And, although the rank and file were relatively inexperienced, the Free State army had in its ranks trained ex-British army officers with experience of leading men and planning strategy from the First World War.

Artillery played an important part in the early stages of the Civil War, and the republicans had none. For most of the Civil War, Liam Lynch, the republican commander-in-chief, had his headquarters in Dublin, and many would argue that, despite his inspirational leadership and intense republican faith, he was out of touch with developments on the ground. Lynch interpreted dissent as bordering on disloyalty, and 'he did not help the Cork IRA by sending three of their key men to posts abroad: Moylan and Leahy were in the USA for most of the war, and Pa Murray became O/C in Britain'.[62] Moylan criticised Lynch's leadership after the defeat at Limerick, and Pa Murray informed Lynch that the war should have ended when Cork fell.

In early 1923, several iconic republican figures were killed in action, captured or surrendered. Dinny Lacey was killed on 18 February; Con Moloney was captured, having been seriously wounded, on 7 March; Dan Breen surrendered without putting up a fight when captured in a dugout on 17 April; and Millstreet battalion Commandant Con Meaney from Cork No. 4 brigade was captured on 21 April. Following these losses and because of the deplorable state of the country, the momentum to stop the fighting increased. The Very Rev. Dr Harty, Archbishop of Cashel and Emly, in consultation with some prominent businessmen and other clergy, put the following proposals to Tom Barry with a request that they would be considered by IRA leaders.

- The immediate cessation of hostilities by calling off all activities and operations by the IRA.
- The dumping of all arms and munitions by the republican forces under the command of the battalion commandants, the battalion commandants to be responsible that the arms will not be used against the Free State government or forces.
- Subsequent to a general election the arms and munitions to be handed over to the elected government of the country.[63]

The group considered the proposals to be of value because they seemed to obviate the difficulty of an unconditional surrender by the republicans. The Very Rev. Canon Tom Duggan, President of St Finbarr's College, Farranferris, Cork, was one of the prime movers behind these proposals. He brought the proposals to Tom Barry who agreed to put them before a meeting of the council of the 1st Southern Division on 10 February. It was decided to request a meeting of the army executive to discuss the proposals. Canon Duggan and Barry travelled to Dublin to present the division's wishes to Liam Lynch.[64] Lynch refused to call an executive meeting to consider the proposals. Barry called to his hideout during the night, but felt that he was poorly received, and during a harsh verbal exchange told Lynch, 'I did more fighting in one week than you did in your whole life!'[65] The peace initiative was rejected, and Barry returned to Cork to form a peace committee. Some of these incidents were published in the press and they must have been well known to the republicans in the field; their effect on morale was devastating.

The debate will rage on as to whether Liam Lynch should have sued for peace in the spring of 1923. However, one thing is certain. His indomitable republican spirit, his absolute faith in the justice of the republican cause, and his unshakeable conviction that the war could be won against all the odds kept republicans fighting when under any other leader they would have faltered.

Liam Lynch finally agreed to hold a meeting of the executive in March 'on Thursday 15th in the 2nd Southern Division area' in the vicinity of Goatenbridge.[66] Due to pressure from Free State forces, the meeting did not start until 24 March. It lasted for four days and, to counter the threat from Free State troops, it was held in several different locations.[67] Éamon de Valera, was present in an adjoining room, 'and was eventually admitted with no voting rights'.[68] Two main resolutions were put to the meeting: they involved either the president entering into negotiations with the Free State government, or a recognition that carrying on the fight would not 'further the cause of independence of the country'. When the voting took place, the result for the first proposal was tied and the second proposal was defeated by one vote – that of Liam Lynch. Consequently, 'it proved impossible to reconcile the divergent views held by members of the executive', and it was decided to meet again for further discussions on 10 April in Araglin, North Cork.[69]

Hopkinson alleges that 'information about the meeting [of the executive] had been extracted from republican prisoners in Dublin'.[70] This would seem unlikely, as Lynch's hideout in Dublin had never been betrayed and his movements up to this point were unknown to the Free State forces. However, the fact that a dispatch rider brought Lynch a 'report from Araglin that a round-up of the area was expected in a day or two',[71] coinciding with the date of the adjourned executive meeting in Araglin, gives some credence to Hopkinson's assertion. Lynch decided to stay in the Newcastle area on the northern slopes of the Knockmealdown Mountains. Hopkinson also alleges that as a result of the receipt of information about Lynch's plans, 'a large sweep was organised under Prout's direction of relevant areas in South Tipperary and Waterford'.[72] The information was not only accurate, but also up-to-date. In the early morning of 10 April, scouts informed Lynch's party that Free State troops were approaching from both east and west. They ran up a shallow stream under temporary cover, but when they emerged onto open ground they came under heavy rifle fire at a range of 300 to 400 yards. After a lull in the firing, 'one single shot rang out. Liam fell. "My God," he said, "I'm hit." He had been seriously wounded.'[73] He died at 8.45 p.m. that evening. Hopkinson states: 'Lynch's death removed the last barrier to a republican acceptance of the need for an end to hostilities.'[74]

Because of Liam Lynch's death, the republican executive did not meet until 20 April. When the meeting was held, 'Frank Aiken succeeded Lynch as chief-of-staff ... and the executive decided to call on de Valera as head of the republican government to make peace with the Free State authorities'.[75] On 27 April, de Valera issued a wordy document announcing the anti-Treaty force's readiness to negotiate a ceasefire. After several days of discussions with government representatives, Senators Jameson and Douglas, de Valera finally proposed that a ceasefire could be achieved if the following proposals were agreed:

- That the sovereign rights of the Irish nation are indefeasible and inalienable.
- No citizen should be excluded from parliament by a political oath.
- There should be strict supervision of arms in the Free State hands.
- Republican forces should have a barracks in each province to store arms that would be controlled by a pledged republican guard.

However, Cosgrave and the Free State government rejected his proposals, mainly because scrapping the oath of allegiance would mean renegotiation of the Treaty and the Constitution.

Also on 27 April, GHQ Dublin notified all commands that 'the army executive at a meeting on the 21.4.23, appointed an army council of three and empowered them, in conjunction with the govt, to make peace with the Free State.' A further order was issued by Chief-of-Staff Frank Aiken, stating, 'you will arrange the suspension of all offensive operations in your area as and from noon 30th April'.[76] Local difficulties must have arisen, because HQ Cork No. 4 brigade found it necessary to issue orders on 15 May that 'O/Cs and all AS units will avoid anything like engagement with the enemy. All aggressive activities must cease forthwith and any officers or men who disobey will be court-martialled.'[77]

Finally, at a joint meeting of the republican government and the army held on 13–14 May, Aiken ordered that 'the arms with which we have fought the enemies of our country are to be dumped. The foreign and domestic enemies of the Republic have for the moment prevailed.' On 24 May 1923, de Valera issued his famous 'proclamation to all ranks of the republican forces':

> Soldiers of Liberty! Legion of the rearguard! The Republic can no longer be defended successfully by your arms. Further sacrifices on your part would now be in vain, and continuance of the struggle in arms unwise in the national interest. Military victory must be allowed to rest for the moment with those who have destroyed the Republic.[78]

Thus, the Civil War ended.

6
Conclusion

Despite political manoeuvring behind the scenes, the Volunteers in the field and many of their leaders had not expected the declaration of the Truce that began on 11 July 1921. They were therefore ill-prepared for its consequences. They had spent two years on the run fighting the might of the British army, with the threat of summary execution hanging over them if they were captured in possession of arms.

The vast majority of the Volunteers were young men plucked from working on the land or from employment as clerks in offices or shops. Some of the officers had second-level education, few had third-level qualifications, and the education of most of the Volunteers would have ended at primary-school level. Their understanding of national freedom was narrow; in essence, it meant the ejection from the country of British troops and the British system of government, and its replacement with a form of government that they believed was free and fundamentally Irish. Consequently, the vast majority of the Volunteers did not have the opportunity to consider the concept of republicanism in any depth, let alone the implications of democracy.

Republicanism for the Volunteers was shorthand for anti-British nationalism, combined with traditional insurrectionism. Republicanism was an expression of Irish identity, and the cry of 'Up the Republic' was hurled provocatively at hated occupying forces. It did not have any philosophical basis, nor did it imply any future structure of government beyond a native Irish government based on self-determination.

In post-First World War Ireland, democracy was sometimes interpreted in different ways. Universal suffrage among males was in its infancy, women did not have the right to vote, and the implications of full civil rights for all had not been addressed. Some people believed that a democratic government based on the will of all the people, male and female, of voting age, was appropriate. But many others believed that government decisions should be based on the general collective will demonstrated over several generations of Irish people, and that doctrines embedded in this general will should influence decision-making in government, even if the expressed will of the majority of the people at a certain point was otherwise. Hence the view that the majority did not have the right to do wrong, i.e. to enforce their own doctrine if it did not agree with that held by several earlier generations, and that a minority who believed in the wishes of the earlier generations had the right to take up arms to vindicate those doctrines against the majority. In this way the republicans could justify taking up arms against the majority of the country because the will of earlier generations had been a complete break from, not the reaching of an accommodation with, Britain.

The Truce put a sudden stop to the War of Independence. Column commandants and officers were no longer the main players. The politicians took centre stage. Young men, for whom survival in kill-or-be-killed situations had been paramount, were lionised as victors against all the odds in a titanic struggle against the 'auld enemy'. However, they had to live with the reality that despite their heightened public profile, they could no longer control the outcome of events. Negotiations would become the order of the day and compromise would have to come into the reckoning if a deal was to be done and a resumption of war avoided.

Éamon de Valera, president of Sinn Féin, the Volunteers and Dáil Éireann, was the logical choice to meet British Prime Minister Lloyd George, to tease out the implications of the Truce. Through meeting Lloyd George and through a public exchange of views in the press, de Valera realised that a republic that rejected the crown was unattainable in the short term. Nevertheless, plenipotentiaries were selected by Dáil Éireann to negotiate a treaty with Britain. De Valera envisaged a collapse in these negotiations and he intended to enter the fray at the last minute so as to avoid war. His final position would be that Ireland should be a republic externally associated with the Empire, recognising the British monarch as the head of the associated states of the Empire. If successful, the integrity of the national republican aspiration would be assured, due recognition would be accorded to the British monarch – thus meeting British requirements – and war would be avoided.

Because of his pre-eminent status and his republican credentials, de Valera was the only person who could have coaxed the doctrinaire republicans into a settlement that had to recognise Britain at some level. When his negotiating strategy collapsed and the cabinet, the Dáil and the people in an election supported the Treaty, de Valera's capacity to influence events was severely curtailed and he played a marginalised role in the unfolding Civil War crisis.

Ultimately, the sticking point for the doctrinaire republicans was the oath of allegiance. They simply could not stomach the swearing of allegiance to a British monarch. Swearing true faith and allegiance to the constitution of the Irish Free State and faithfulness to the British monarch in virtue of the common citizenship of Ireland with Great Britain, was seen as fudging the issue and incompatible with the pure, undefiled republicanism of the 1916 Rising and the historical republican heritage. Doctrines embedded in the general will of generations of Irish republicans were invoked; the majority could not betray that precious trust and civil war to vindicate that trust became inevitable.

The young men of the IRA had to choose. The interminable wrangling in the Dáil debates and complicated proposals such as external association were beyond them; practically to a man, they followed the choice of their senior officers and supported the Provisional Government or the anti-Treaty faction depending on them. The seizure of the Four Courts by republicans was highly symbolic and epitomised all that was held dear about the 1916 Rising. However, it distracted the republicans from building a unified force under an effective and unified central command with clear, well-thought-out strategies. The crisis sharpened the focus of the Provisional Government, bought it time to build an army with considerable military resources and stiffened its determination to fight for the Treaty, a decision that was supported by the electorate on 16 June 1922. The capture of the Four Courts and the subsequent defeat of republicans in central Dublin handed a badly needed victory to the Provisional Government, proving that their forces had the capacity to defeat republican forces that were generally perceived to be militarily superior because of their achievements in the War of Independence. The victory raised the morale of the raw recruits in the Free State army and, correspondingly, was a blow to republican morale.

Despite the appointment of the experienced fighter Liam Lynch as commander-in-chief of the republican forces, there seemed to be little coherent strategy or any clear line of command in the republican forces. Ernie O'Malley made the decision to defend Blessington and he also decided to pull out following the initial attack on the town by pro-Treaty forces. Seán Moylan decided to descend upon Wexford with 230 men to bolster the defence of the south-east. He also decided to retreat without engaging pro-Treaty forces. Neither seemed to be operating under the orders of the CIC, and their decisions seem to have been taken on an *ad hoc* basis. Dan Breen and Dinny Lacey failed to attack Prout's rear when Waterford was being shelled, and Pa Murray did not arrive with a Cork column to relieve that hard-pressed city. These men were experienced leaders with outstanding War of

Independence records, and the men under their command were seasoned fighters. In the War of Independence, of necessity, they operated with little reference to superior officers. However, in the Civil War, coordinated planning under a unified command was essential to defeat the pro-Treaty commander, General Prout – a man with British army training and experience, backed by a weak but single-minded government. A major republican weakness was being exposed.

Emmet Dalton – another general with extensive British army war experience – quickly realised that it would be extremely difficult to capture the Four Courts without artillery. Eighteen-pounder field guns were thus obtained from the British, and the Four Courts fell within days. The republicans should have learned from this experience about the physical and psychological effect incoming artillery fire can have on troops operating in defensive positions who have never experienced shell fire and are unprepared for such fire. Their command should also have planned for how to counteract such fire.

Holding Waterford and Limerick cities was crucial to the defence of the 'Munster Republic'. Yet Waterford city was captured with relative ease, having being shelled by one eighteen-pounder operating from Mount Misery on the northern side of the river. No attempt was made by republicans to neutralise this gun and no attack was made on the gunners from the rear. Although Limerick proved a harder nut to crack, once the shells began to land on the Ordnance and Strand barracks, it was obvious to republicans that their positions were untenable. Again, a single artillery piece was allowed to shell the city with impunity. Limerick was evacuated on 21 July 1922 and republicans freely admitted this evacuation had a serious effect on morale. Pro-Treaty morale grew proportionately.

The republicans decided to make another stand at Kilmallock. The town was an excellent strong-point, in that it was surrounded by four low hills. If the outer defences were breached, machine-gun emplacements on these hills would enable defenders to enfilade attacking forces in a devastating crossfire. General W.R.E. Murphy – another ex-British army officer with extensive First World War experience – prepared the plan to attack Kilmallock; it was predicated on capturing the four hills with concentrated artillery fire. The first shrapnel shells that landed in the depression on Quarry Hill killed and scattered men and machine-guns alike. The shelling continued with devastating effect on the three other hills, softening up or neutralising republican positions with impunity. Despite previous experience, no effort had been made to prepare positions for defence against artillery, and, again, no effort was made to silence the gun or even reduce its efficacy through sniping. Kilmallock was evacuated within twenty-four hours. In summary, in the early stages of the Civil War, the skilful use of field artillery gave the pro-Treaty forces a decided advantage everywhere republicans tried to make a stand in a fixed position.

Poor strategic planning and simmering discontent with the senior republican command weakened the defence of Limerick. Commander-in-Chief Liam Lynch must have known in late June and early July that pro-Treaty forces had defeated the republicans in Dublin and in Blessington. Yet despite being in a dominant position in Limerick, he not only refused to attack weak pro-Treaty positions, he concluded two local truce agreements with General Brennan, the pro-Treaty commander. His subordinates were incensed at the lack of attacking policies, as delays allowed the pro-Treaty forces to bring in reinforcements and supplies. Lynch's decision to leave Limerick and transfer his headquarters to Clonmel was equally inexplicable, and did not bolster the morale of his troops. Dissension spilled over into Kilmallock.

There is evidence that republican O/C Liam Deasy did not have full control over his forces and that one Limerick column refused to operate under Cork Command. If the intelligence of the pro-Treaty force attacking Kilmallock is accurate, a force of 1,000 republicans was operating south of Kilmallock within striking distance of the town. A force of half that number would have been sufficient to relieve the siege of Kilmallock if they were under a disciplined and coordinated central command. Yet no relieving force arrived. When Kilmallock had been evacuated, the Kerry brigades were 'ordered to withdraw' to Kerry. This command must have come from someone other than Liam Lynch and local O/C Liam Deasy had no say in the decision. An uncoordinated republican command structure – albeit with good-quality troops under its command – was no match for a unified pro-Treaty command with troops of lesser experience and training. Once the word got out that Free State forces had landed at Fenit the commandant of Kerry No. 1 Brigade, John Joe Sheehy, would have felt free to pull his men out and return to defend Kerry without recourse to senior officers.

The fall of Kilmallock precipitated a headlong retreat southwards of republican forces. Between 4 August and 19 August, pro-Treaty forces occupied every significant town and village in north Munster, with minimal republican resistance. The order to vacate barracks and form columns was first issued verbally, then confirmed in writing by Liam Deasy on 12 August, and further confirmed by Liam Lynch on 19 August. The sequence confirms the republican command problems. CIC Liam Lynch should have been issuing these orders and at no stage should verbal orders with serious future strategic implications have been issued at lower or local levels. Lack of clarity in command coupled with an inability to engage pro-Treaty forces in delaying actions had a demoralising effect on republicans, while pro-Treaty morale and prestige were enhanced by the occupation of the towns and the benefits of the facilities available there.

Republicans strove to regroup in columns of twenty-four men using familiar guerrilla tactics. Yet in County Cork, only two brigades made a relatively successful transition: Cork No. 4 and

Cork No. 5 brigades. Cork No. 4 brigade, under the command of Commandant Paddy O'Brien of Liscarroll, dominated the rural areas of North Cork in the autumn and early winter of 1922. The guerrilla columns were highly successful, if success is measured by keeping pro-Treaty forces pinned in the towns and the wrecking of surrounding infrastructure and the communications networks. These tactics, and particularly large-scale attacks on towns such as Newmarket and Millstreet, undermined the stability of the Provisional Government in the area and the confidence of the people in their capacity to govern, and were a severe setback for the pro-Treaty forces that had occupied the towns with comparative ease in August. Yet the republicans failed to capitalise on their successes.

A number of factors combined to bring an end to the Civil War in North Cork and throughout the country. The republicans gradually lost the good will of the people by their tactics. Destruction of infrastructure seriously inconvenienced rural communities and the attacks on the railways angered people throughout the country. These activities were tolerable in the War of Independence against a common enemy, but were adjudged to be futile in an internecine struggle. The pro-Treaty force's well-planned, regular, large-scale sweeps and local round-ups gradually reduced guerrilla activity. Continuous harassment of republicans in their strongholds produced many arrests. The full power and panoply of the Catholic Church was brought to bear against the republicans, and clerical denouncements held great weight in church-going communities.

However, a most telling blow was delivered to republicans when the Dáil gave the army special powers to inflict the death penalty on men caught in possession of firearms without proper authority. While commentators consider the seventy-seven executions a serious blot on the record of the Free State government, most agree that this action hastened the end of the Civil War. The additional policy of suspending death sentences on individuals on condition that hostilities ended in the local communities of sentenced men, placed intolerable pressure on the republicans in those communities and greatly restricted their activities.

The capture of Liam Deasy, republican DCS, was a severe blow in itself to republicans, but his subsequent signing of an appeal to the republican leadership to surrender unconditionally had a devastating effect on the republican campaign in North Cork and countrywide. Its effect can be gauged by the panic orders issued by the Cork No. 4 Command threatening dire consequences against republicans who surrendered. The appeal also gave rise to numerous requests by prisoners for release to propose cessation of republican activities, together with an increase in voluntary surrenders to pro-Treaty forces countrywide. It also generated the expectation in Munster that the war would be concluded in a short time.

In North Cork, and particularly in the Charleville area, the attrition wrought on the republican columns by Ned Cronin, commandant of Free State forces based in Charleville, proved decisive. Throughout the spring of 1923, his forces raided republican haunts almost on a daily basis. His battalion outnumbered and out-gunned the forces of republican Commandant Paddy O'Brien, and pro-Treaty raids continued until republican morale was severely depleted and they were rendered ineffective. A similar situation occurred in the Mallow area. By May, all officers of the 5th battalion had been captured, and remaining Volunteers had deserted or resigned.

The circumstances surrounding the death of Liam Lynch encapsulate the tragedy of the Civil War. He was mortally wounded by a single shot while trying to evade capture with Frank Aiken and Seán Hyde on the northern slopes of the Knockmealdown Mountains. It was a lonely end for an indefatigable and inspirational leader whose faith in the doctrinaire republican ideal had remained constant in the face of insurmountable difficulties and looming republican defeat. His death opened the way for an end to hostilities and the eventual cessation of the Civil War.

The general surveys issued for the North Cork area to the Limerick Free State Command confirmed the gradual petering-out of the war and the growing support for the Free State army. The report for the week ending 10 May says:

> There has been a marked decrease in the Irregular activities all over the command for the past few weeks ... outside the immediate relatives and friends of the Irregulars, and a few hysterical members of Cumann na mBan, everybody endorses the action of the government and the army.[1]

In Shandrum parish, the Free State soldiers guarded 'polling booths for the general election held on 27/8/23' and 'did not accept sympathy with any party ... nor pass comments on election or impersonating agents nor any of the electors', and 'public houses and hotels were out of bounds to all troops all day'.[2] Consequently, the general survey for the period ending 17 October 1923 could note that 'the election passed off very quietly. There were no disturbances of any kind worthy of mention.'[3] The report stated that 'Irregular organisation in this command is still being carried on'. However, the report ended on a positive note: 'From all parts come very favourable reports as to the attitude of the people generally towards our troops.' It added: 'There is no doubt but the uniform of the National Army is much more popular now than it used to be', and 'people are at last beginning to realise that the soldiers of the National Army are the friends and protectors of the people rather than the representatives of military tyranny as they were formerly led to believe'.[4]

Hopkinson concludes: 'The Treaty and the Civil War period had posed important and intractable questions about the causation and interpretation of events'[5] both before and during the war. Irrespective of the causes posited for the Civil War, or the main players and their roles, once the Treaty was accepted by a majority of the people, it was unavoidable and imperative that the Provisional Government asserted its authority. Hopkinson suggests that 'only a political compromise on the constitutional issues could have averted fighting and that was unrealisable'.[6] Therefore, as Younger says, 'if they were to govern they had to eliminate acts of violence throughout the country, armed opposition to the functions of government and the illegal occupation of public buildings'.[7]

The alternative was a tame abdication of the mandate given to it by the people, potential rule by military dictatorship, the vindication of the principle that a dissenting minority had the right to achieve its ends through arms and, ultimately, chaos. The crucible of the Civil War forged an unshakable conviction in the hearts of the people of the Free State that war was not the way to resolve intractable issues among themselves or, more importantly, between the Free State and the dominant majority in Northern Ireland. As Younger says, 'what had at last been established was that the army was an instrument of the government, the government not a weapon of the army, that the revolution was complete and power belonged in the hands of the people'.[8]

The Irish people have proved themselves worthy of the power entrusted to them. In retrospect, this outcome alone may, incongruously, have made the blood sacrifices of the Civil War worthwhile.

Appendix
Main Characters and Events

1916 Rising

On Easter Monday, 24 April 1916, members of the Irish Volunteers, led by Patrick Pearse, and members of the Irish Citizen Army, led by James Connolly, seized key locations in the centre of Dublin. Patrick Pearse read the Proclamation of the Republic outside the General Post Office in what is now O'Connell Street. The fighting lasted for six days, but on the Saturday, Pearse drafted a general order to surrender so as 'to prevent the further slaughter of Dublin citizens, and in the hope of saving the lives of our followers now surrounded and hopelessly outnumbered.' The leaders were court-martialled and executed. Militarily, the Rising was a failure. However, the execution of its leaders outraged many people and became a significant factor in the subsequent rise of militant Irish nationalism.[1]

Ard Fheis

The ard fheis was a national gathering of representatives of the Sinn Féin organisation. The ard fheis was usually held in the Mansion House, Dublin, where the president was elected and policy decisions and other matters were debated.[2]

Army Convention

The anti-Treaty members of the IRA wished to hold an army convention to set up an independent army executive outside the control of the minister for defence. Eventually, the convention was held on 26 March 1922, despite an order banning it issued by Griffith on 16 March. The convention reaffirmed the republican status of the army and agreed that the army should be brought back under the control of an executive appointed by the convention. The convention showed the extent of the split in the army, and the anti-Treaty IRA were now cut off from the Provisional Government and financial support.[3]

Dick Barrett

A committed republican. He was quartermaster of Cork No. 3 brigade. He was captured when the Four Courts garrison surrendered on 30 June 1922 in the first action of the Civil War. He was executed on 8 December 1922 as a reprisal for the killing of Seán Hales in Dublin in an ambush laid by the Dublin anti-Treaty IRA.[4]

Tom Barry

Commander of Cork No. 3 flying column. He was a British army veteran, a belligerent and brilliant leader, and led the West Cork column at its famed Kilmichael ambush in November 1920 and during the break-out from encircling British forces at Crossbarry. Barry joined the militant faction of the anti-Treaty IRA, though in early 1923 changed his position and advocated peace. His classic memoir is entitled *Guerrilla Days in Ireland*.[5]

Robert C. Barton

A cousin of Erskine Childers, he was born into a Protestant landowning family in County Wicklow. A nationalist who served with the British in the war, he converted to Sinn Féin after the Easter Rising. He was a delegate to the Treaty conference in 1921, and though a republican, he was won over by the arguments of his colleagues to sign the Treaty. He voted with Griffith against de Valera in the cabinet of 7 December 1921, but refused later to cooperate with the Provisional Government.[6]

Break on the North

The Government of Ireland Act 1920 established a separate government in Northern Ireland. The Dáil government at that time claimed to govern all thirty-two counties. Doctrinaire republicans considered Northern Ireland an integral part of the Irish state. In the negotiations that followed the Truce in 1921, Éamon de Valera instructed the Irish plenipotentiaries to ensure that if the negotiations broke down, the breaking point should be the issue of the unacceptability for nationalists of a separate unionist state in Northern Ireland.[7]

Dan Breen

A staunch republican and fearless freedom fighter, he was sworn into the IRB by his friend and fellow republican, Seán Treacy. He was a member of the Irish Volunteers and in the company of Treacy, Seamus Robinson and Seán Hogan when the first shots of the War of Independence were fired on 21 January 1919. In an ambush to acquire explosives, they shot dead two RIC men at Soloheadbeg. He became a celebrated gunman with a price of £10,000 on his head and he participated in many actions, including the rescue of Seán Hogan at Knocklong and the ambush of Lord French at Ashtown. He supported the anti-Treaty IRA in the Civil War and, while prepared to fight to the finish, he believed that peace should have been considered in the spring of 1923.[8]

Michael Brennan

IRA commandant of the 1st Western Division, he was a supporter of the Treaty and the Provisional Government commandant of Limerick in 1922. He fought on the pro-Treaty side of the Civil War.[9]

Cathal Brugha

Dáil minister for defence 1919–22. Brugha gained fame for his heroism during the 1916 Rising when he single-handedly held a position against British troops despite being critically wounded. He was overshadowed in the IRA by Michael Collins and Richard Mulcahy. He opposed the Anglo-Irish Treaty and sided with Éamon de Valera. During the opening days of the Civil War Brugha was killed in Dublin, after making a brave but suicidal one-man charge against a group of Free State soldiers.[10]

Robert Erskine Childers

Born of an English father and an Irish mother, but brought up by the Barton family in County Wicklow. He organised the Howth gun-running in 1914. Served in the Royal Navy 1915–17 and won the DSO for gallantry. Left the navy to work for Irish freedom. A passionate republican, he was secretary of the Irish delegation in 1921. Joined de Valera in repudiating the Treaty. Fought with the republicans in the Civil War and was captured and executed for possession of firearms in November 1922.[11]

Michael Collins

The War of Independence's most celebrated leader. The West Cork native spent his early adulthood in London working as a bank and postal clerk. There, Sam Maguire introduced Collins to the GAA, Irish cultural groups and eventually the Irish Republican

Brotherhood. Collins returned to Dublin to fight in the Easter Rising and emerged from the prison camps in Frongoch, Wales, as a key leader in the Volunteer movement. He subsequently headed the IRB, organised the IRA's intelligence department and served as the Dáil minister for finance. A leader of the Irish delegation to the Anglo-Irish Treaty negotiations, he championed the agreement and was largely responsible for its passage. The first chairman of the Free State Provisional Government, he took charge of the Irish army at the outbreak of the Civil War. On 22 August 1922, he was killed during an ambush of his convoy while he toured West Cork.[12]

Cork No. 4 Brigade

On 10 July, while considering the implications of the impending Truce, it was decided by the Divisional O/C Liam Lynch to divide North Cork into two brigade areas. George Power was to continue to command Cork No. 2 brigade and Paddy O'Brien was appointed O/C Cork No. 4 brigade.[13]

Sir James Craig

Born in Belfast, he fought in south-west Africa in the First World War. Carson's lieutenant in the pre-1914 struggle against Irish home rule, he organised resistance in the North. First Prime Minister of Northern Ireland under Government of Ireland Act 1921.[14]

Liam Deasy

Commander of Cork No. 3 brigade. Deasy succeeded Charlie Hurley as O/C of the West Cork brigade in the spring of 1921 and also served as Cork's IRB secretary. After the Truce in July 1921, Deasy joined the 1st Southern Division as vice-commander and later commanded the unit. During the Civil War, he was promoted to anti-Treaty IRA deputy chief-of-staff. After his capture in early 1923, Deasy issued a unilateral call for surrender, which caused considerable dissension and morale problems in IRA ranks.[15]

Éamon de Valera

President of Sinn Féin and Dáil Éireann from 1918–22. The former mathematics teacher was the long-time taoiseach and president of Ireland. After his escape from Lincoln jail in early 1919, de Valera spent the next two years in America raising funds. He rejected the Anglo-Irish Treaty and took the republican side in the Civil War. De Valera founded the Fianna Fáil party in 1926 and led its first government in 1932. He was the dominant Irish political figure of the twentieth century, heading many Fianna Fáil governments. He was elected president of Ireland in 1959, serving two terms until his retirement in 1972.[16]

George Gavan Duffy

A son of one of the organisers of the Young Ireland movement of the 1840s, Duffy was a successful solicitor in London. A delegate to the Treaty conference in 1921, he was the last to agree to sign the Treaty. Appointed by Griffith as minister for foreign affairs in the Dáil cabinet of 1922.[17]

Free State

On 25 October 1922, the Dáil passed the Free State Constitution Bill. On 6 December the House of Commons passed the corresponding bill and the Irish Free State came into being.[18]

David Lloyd George

Trained as a lawyer he became a leading figure of British politics. A Liberal MP from 1890–1945, Chancellor of the Exchequer 1908–15, secretary for war, 1916, and prime minister 1916–22, he led the British side in the Treaty negotiations in 1921.[19]

Arthur Griffith

Skilled propagandist, founder of Sinn Féin and the intellectual leader of the independence movement. From 1919–20, Griffith acted as Dáil president during Éamon de Valera's absence in America. With Michael Collins, Griffith led the Anglo-Irish Treaty negotiations and later championed the Treaty. He subsequently succeeded de Valera as president of Dáil Éireann and served as the de facto president of the Irish Free State. Overworked and stressed by the outbreak of the Civil War, Griffith died of a cerebral haemorrhage in August 1922.[20]

Seán Hales

The brother of Tom Hales, who founded the Volunteer organisation in the Bandon area. He commanded the Bandon battalion Cork No. 3 brigade. He took the pro-Treaty side in the Civil War and was a Free State army general and pro-Treaty TD. He was assassinated as retaliation for the execution of IRA prisoners in 1922 and because he voted for the 'Murder Bill'. His death prompted the Free State's execution of Liam Mellows, Joe McKelvey, Rory O'Connor and Dick Barrett.[21]

Internal/External self-determination

In its appeal to President Wilson on 5 November 1918, the Irish Parliamentary Party defined self-determination as 'all nations, large and small, should have free self-determination as to their form of government and that no people should be ruled and dominated even in their own internal affairs by arbitrary and irresponsible force instead of their own will and choice'. The external version of the doctrine implies a right for people to choose the sovereignty under which they live, whereas the internal version means the right of people to choose their own form of government.[22]

Irish Volunteers (Óglaigh na hÉireann)
Founded in November 1913. A split occurred when the Volunteers were urged by John Redmond to support Britain in the First World War during his Woodenbridge speech of 20 September 1914. The majority, renamed the National Volunteers, sided with Redmond, while the minority, the Irish Volunteers, reorganised with a separatist nationalist agenda. During 1915, the National Volunteers crumbled and the Irish Volunteer force began to rebuild its strength countrywide. The Irish Volunteers participated in the 1916 Rising and large numbers from many parishes were interned in Wales. By 1918 the whole of the County Cork Volunteers had been reorganised under Tomás MacCurtain into a brigade consisting of twenty battalions, each with an average of eight parish-based companies.[23]

June Election 1922
In May 1922 Collins and de Valera met for three days. The result of their negotiations was that a national coalition panel for the coming election would be formed. The proportion of the candidates chosen for the panel would be according to their strength in the Dáil. Following the election, a coalition executive would be formed. The agreement suited de Valera in that it afforded him an opportunity to regroup and avoid a serious electoral defeat. It suited Collins and the Provisional Government in that it meant the election would take place, that it would slow the slide to civil

war, that it would give breathing space for the drafting of the new constitution, and give the Provisional Government time to re-build the machinery of state, including an army. The election was held on 16 June, resulting in a heavy defeat for the republicans.[24]

Kilkenny Standoff

In early May 1922 anti-Treaty forces in Kilkenny took over various positions in the city, including Ormond Castle and the city hall. The Provisional Government sent 200 men from the Dublin Guard by train to Kilkenny, and they retook the buildings. Amid exchanges of fire, an arrangement was patched together in Dublin whereby the barracks in the city were shared by the rival IRA forces. Outright military confrontation was avoided.[25]

Dinny Lacey

Tipperary republican and friend of Dan Breen. Joined the Irish Volunteers with Breen and Treacy. Led the famous south Tipperary column in the War of Independence. He supported the anti-Treaty side in the Civil War and was killed early in 1923 in a gun battle with Free State forces while on a mission to discuss ceasefire proposals from the neutral IRA Men's Association.[26]

Limerick Crisis

British forces began to evacuate Limerick in late February 1922. Rival units of pro-Treaty and anti-Treaty IRA jockeyed to take over strategic buildings in Limerick city. The opposing forces were slow to initiate hostilities despite Arthur Griffith's belief that the republican strongholds should be attacked and taken. A temporary local truce was negotiated by Liam Lynch and Michael Brennan at the instigation of Mayor O'Mara and all-out hostilities were postponed until June and July 1922.[27]

Liam Lynch

Commander of Cork No. 2 brigade, O/C of the 1st Southern Division and chief-of-staff of the anti-Treaty IRA. He led some of his brigades' most successful sorties in the War of Independence, including the capture of General Lucas and an assault on British soldiers going to church in Fermoy. A capable administrator, Lynch impressed colleagues with his unwavering dedication to the republican cause, which seemed almost religious in its intensity. Lynch became the primary republican leader during the Civil War. He led the anti-Treaty IRA forces until his death at the hands of Free State troops in the Knockmealdown Mountains on 10 April 1923.[28]

Archbishop Daniel Mannix

Daniel Mannix, native of Charleville, County Cork was Catholic archbishop of Melbourne; he was a staunch Sinn Féin supporter. While he supported many of the aims and objectives of the republicans, he reluctantly supported the Treaty.[29]

General Sir Nevil Macready

Commander of the British forces in Belfast 1914; adjutant general to the forces 1916–18; commissioner of police of the metropolis, 1918–20; commander-in-chief of the British forces in Ireland, March 1920–22.[30]

Joe McKelvey

Commander of the Belfast brigade and an anti-Treaty IRA leader. McKelvey helped organise the assassination of District Inspector Swanzy in Lisburn. Swanzy was believed to be implicated in the murder of Tomás MacCurtain, lord mayor of Cork. McKelvey was a key opponent of the Anglo-Irish Treaty within both the IRB and the anti-Treaty IRA's militant faction. He was captured when the Four Courts fell and was executed by the Free State government as a reprisal for the assassination of pro-Treaty TD Seán Hales.[31]

Seán McKeown

Blacksmith of Ballinalee, leader of a Volunteer band and commandant of the IRA's Midland Division. An old ally of Collins, he was captured and sentenced to death, but released during the Truce in August 1921. A supporter of the Treaty, he fought on the Free State side during the Civil War.[32]

Con Meaney

A staunch republican and a member of the IRB. He was instrumental in reviving and reorganising the Volunteers in the Millstreet area. During the War of Independence, he was O/C of the 7th battalion Cork No. 2 brigade and subsequently O/C of the 1st battalion Cork No. 4 brigade. He took part in all engagements with the British forces in the area, including the ambushes at Clonbanin and Rathcool. He fought with the republican side in the Civil War.[33]

Liam Mellows

Born in England, the son of a British army sergeant. Came to live in Ireland in 1895 and became interested in the national struggle for independence. Joined Fianna Éireann and the Irish Volunteers. Elected TD for Galway in the first and second Dáil. He took the republican side in the Civil War, was captured and imprisoned following the surrender of the Four Courts at the end of June 1922. He was executed in Mountjoy jail on 8 December 1922 as a reprisal for the shooting of Seán Hales TD.[34]

Con Moloney

Republican and close friend of Liam Lynch. During the War of Independence, he was brigade adjutant of the 3rd Tipperary brigade. Supported the anti-Treaty side in the Civil War and became adjutant general to Liam Lynch. He put tentative proposals to Liam Lynch in March 1923 to end the Civil War, but Lynch rejected them. He was wounded and captured after a fight in the Glen of Aherlow on 7 March 1923.[35]

Seán Moylan

Prominent leader and successful flying column commander of the Cork No. 2 brigade. Moylan led his column to victories at Tureengarriffe and Clonbanin, and succeeded Liam Lynch as O/C Cork No. 2 brigade. As a TD, he voted against the Anglo-Irish Treaty and was associated with the 1st Southern Division's moderate faction during the run-up to the Civil War. After the Civil War, Moylan enjoyed a long career as a Fianna Fáil TD and minister for lands.[36]

General W.R.E. Murphy

Second-in-command to General Eoin O'Duffy, GOC South-Western Command. He was a British army veteran who led offensives during the First World War. He prepared the plans for the attack on the town of Kilmallock on 4 August 1922. He commanded pro-Treaty forces in Kerry up to January 1923. He was highly regarded as an efficient general officer.[37]

Patrick 'Pa' Murray

Commander of the Cork city active service unit and leader of many ambushes and attacks. He commanded IRA forces in Cork city during 1921 and kept them active despite intense British pressure. Murray earlier headed an assassination team sent to London to kill members of the British cabinet during Terence MacSwiney's hunger strike. He also led the shooting team that tracked down the informer 'Croxy' O'Connor in New York city in early 1922. During the Civil War, he sided with the anti-Treaty forces and became the IRA's O/C Britain.[38]

Paddy O'Brien

Commander of Cork No. 4 brigade from before the Truce until the end of the Civil War. A staunch republican, he fought in all the notable engagements against the British forces during the War of Independence. He took the republican side in the Civil War and because of his inspired leadership North Cork was one of the most troublesome areas for Free State forces up to the order to cease fire and dump arms on 24 May 1923.[39]

Rory O'Connor

A republican and a member of the IRB, he took part in the Easter Rising. He fought with Collins as director of engineering of the IRA, was in charge of subversive operations in England and was one of those who occupied the Four Courts in Dublin in 1922. He was captured and later shot in Mountjoy jail on 8 December 1922 as a reprisal for the shooting of Seán Hales TD.[40]

Florence O'Donoghue

Born near Rathmore, County Kerry, he went to work in Cork city as a youth. Joined the Volunteers in 1917, was promoted to first lieutenant quickly, and in April 1917 was sworn into the IRB. He founded the brigade cyclist company and was appointed brigade O/C communications and brigade adjutant in 1918. He had a reputation for being a shrewd, calm and capable officer. He organised the breakout of Denis MacNeilus from Cork jail in November 1918. He was appointed brigade intelligence officer, and set up a highly effective intelligence system in the brigade area. Prior to the outbreak of the Civil War, he was promoted to adjutant general of the anti-Treaty IRA. Along with Seán O'Hegarty, he remained neutral during the Civil War, and was involved in many attempts to end the conflict. He became a respected commentator and author on all aspects of the Civil War and the War of Independence. His best-known books are *No Other Law*, a biography of Liam Lynch, and *Tomás MacCurtain*, a biography of the murdered lord mayor of Cork.[41]

General Eoin O'Duffy

O'Duffy was an active member of the IRA during the War of Independence and was elected to the second Dáil for the Monaghan constituency in the 1921 general election. He voted in favour of the Anglo-Irish Treaty and supported the pro-Treaty side in the Civil War. He was GOC South-Western Command of the pro-Treaty forces in July 1922, and successfully attacked Limerick and Kilmallock, routing the anti-Treaty IRA forces. He was instrumental in reorganising the Civic Guard and was appointed commissioner of *An Garda Síochána* in 1924 when the Civil War had ended.[42]

Peter O'Farrell

O'Farrell joined the Irish Volunteers at its inception in the Charleville area. He was an active Volunteer throughout the War of Independence, taking part in many actions of the flying column of Cork No. 2 brigade. He took the republican side in the Civil War, and fought with Cork No. 4 brigade at Quarry Hill in the battle for Kilmallock.[43]

P.S. O'Hegarty

Patrick Sarsfield O'Hegarty was a founder of Sinn Féin and an effective republican propagandist. The brother of Seán O'Hegarty, Patrick managed the Cork post office until his dismissal for republican activities. He remained close to Arthur Griffith, supported the Anglo-Irish Treaty, and became the Irish Free State's first postmaster general. The author of numerous books and academic articles, his work, *The Victory of Sinn Féin*, was an early first-hand account of the independence struggle.[44]

Seán O'Hegarty

Commander of Cork No. 1 brigade. The pugnacious, opinionated and strict leader succeeded Terence MacSwiney as brigade O/C in August 1920. He brought discipline and an aggressive fighting spirit to the brigade, but frequently feuded with GHQ leaders in Dublin. In the run-up to the Civil War, O'Hegarty gained head-lines by organising the capture of the British arms ship *Upnor*, threatening the lives of pro-Treaty TDs and abducting a hostile British journalist. However, O'Hegarty stayed neutral during the Civil War and, with Florrie O'Donoghue, worked to negotiate an end to the conflict.[45]

Ernie O'Malley

O'Malley was a medical student in Trinity College, Dublin when the Easter Rising began. He became deeply involved in Irish republicanism, and worked as a full-time organiser for the IRA. He took part in many actions during the War of Independence, including the capture of Mallow barracks in September 1920. As commandant of the 2nd Southern Division, he rejected the Treaty and joined the republican side in the Civil War. He was deputy chief-of-staff to Liam Lynch and O/C Northern and Eastern Command of the anti-Treaty IRA. He was captured after a shootout with Free State forces in November 1922, but the severity of his wounds saved him from execution. His account of the War of Independence, *On Another Man's Wound*, was critically acclaimed, and his views on the Civil War are outlined in his memoir, *The Singing Flame*.[46]

General J.T. Prout

Prout was appointed GOC South-Eastern Command of the pro-Treaty forces in early July. Despite a cautious approach, he captured Waterford, Carrick-on-Suir and Clonmel. He held the command until the end of the Civil War.[47]

Provisional Government

Until the legislation setting up the Free State could be passed, both in the British parliament and in the Dáil, a Provisional Government was established. The only authority for the Provisional Government's existence was the Treaty. As long as the second Dáil and the Dáil government remained in existence, the constitutional authority of the Provisional Government was disputed by republicans.[48]

Sinn Féin

A political organisation founded by Arthur Griffith. In time, the name Sinn Féin came to be applied to all republicans and all organisations with national aspirations gathered under its banner. In the October ard fheis of 1917, a constitution was adopted declaring that Sinn Féin aimed at securing the international recognition of Ireland as an independent Irish Republic. In the 1918 election, seventy-three nationalists were elected under the Sinn Féin banner. They met in the Mansion House and decided to abstain from Westminster and form a government under President Éamon de Valera.[49]

Austin Stack

A Fenian by birth and upbringing, he took part in the Easter Rising. Minister for home affairs in the Dáil cabinet of 1919–21, he refused to join the delegation to London. He voted with de Valera against the Treaty. The most uncompromising of the republicans.[50]

Upnor

The *Upnor* was a British Admiralty ship due to leave Haulbowline dockyard, Queenstown, for Portsmouth with a cargo of small arms and ammunition. On 31 March 1922, the anti-Treaty IRA commandeered the tug *Warrior* at Queenstown, intercepted the *Upnor* at sea and diverted it to Ballycotton harbour. There, the arms – mainly rifles and revolvers – were loaded onto a fleet of commandeered lorries and cars, and distributed to Munster anti-Treaty IRA units. The haul is estimated to have included 1,500 rifles, 55 Lewis guns and 500,000 rounds of .303 ammunition.[51]

Notes & References

Prologue: The End of the War of Independence in North Cork

1   Younger, Calton, *Ireland's Civil War* (1968), p. 152.

2   *Ibid.*, p. 153.

3   *Ibid.*, p. 154.

4   M/A, witness statement, Comdt Paddy O'Brien.

5   O'Donoghue, Florence, *No Other Law* (1986), p. 18.

Chapter 1: Build-up to the Civil War

1   Younger, Calton, *Ireland's Civil War* (1968), p. 35.

2   *Ibid.*, p. 42.

3   *Ibid.*, p. 44.

4   Lee, J.J., *Ireland 1912–1985: Politics and Society* (1989), p. 38.

5   *Ibid.*

6   Younger, Calton, *Ireland's Civil War* (1968), p. 80.

7   Hopkinson, Michael, *Green Against Green* (1988), p. 23.

8   Curran, J.M., *The Birth of the Irish Free State 1921–1923* (1980), p. 59.

9   Hopkinson, Michael, *Green Against Green* (1988), p. 23.

10   Lee, J.J., *Ireland 1912–1985: Politics and Society* (1989), p. 48, quoting M. Moynihan (ed.), *Speeches and Statements by Éamon de Valera 1917–73* (Dublin: Gill & Macmillan, 1980), p. 70.

11   Lee, J.J., *Ireland 1912–1985* (1989), p. 48.

12   Regan, J.M., *The Irish Counter-revolution 1921–1936: Treatyite Politics and Settlement in Independent Ireland* (1999), p. 10.

13   *Ibid.*

14   Lee, J.J., *Ireland 1912–1985* (1989), p. 49.

15   Hopkinson, Michael, *Green Against Green* (1988), p. 24.

16   O'Hegarty, P.S., *The Victory of Sinn Féin* (1998), p. 47.

17   Lee, J.J., *Ireland 1912–1985* (1989), p. 47.

18   *Cork Examiner,* 13 & 14 July 1921.

19   Hopkinson, Michael, *Green Against Green* (1988), p. 24.

20   Curran, J.M., *The Birth of the Irish Free State* (1980), p. 71.

21   Lee, J.J., *Ireland 1912–1985* (1989), p. 48.

22   *Ibid.*

23   *Cork Examiner,* 17 July 1921.

24   *Cork Examiner,* 16 July 1921.

25   *Cork Examiner,* 17 July 1921.

26   *Cork Examiner,* 19 July 1921.

27   Younger, Calton, *Ireland's Civil War* (1968), p. 154.

28   Curran, J.M., *The Birth of the Irish Free State* (1980), p. 59.

29   Hopkinson, Michael, *Green Against Green* (1988), p. 23.

30   *Cork Examiner,* 26 Sept. 1921.

31   Lee, J.J., *Ireland 1912–1985* (1989), p. 48.

32   Regan, J.M., *The Irish Counter-revolution* (1999), p. 5.

33   Younger, Calton, *Ireland's Civil War* (1968), p. 156.

34   *Ibid.*, p. 147.

35   *Ibid.*

36   Regan, J.M., The *Irish Counter-revolution* (1999), p. 13.

37   *Ibid.*

38   *Ibid.*

39   Kissane, Bill, *The Politics of the Irish Civil War* (2005), p. 54.

40   Regan, J.M., *The Irish Counter-revolution* (1999), p. 15.

41   Hopkinson, Michael, *Green Against Green* (1988), p. 35.

42   Lawlor, Sheila, *Britain and Ireland* (1983), p. 147.

43   Regan, J.M., *The Irish Counter-revolution* (1999), p. 15.

44   Hopkinson, Michael, *Green Against Green* (1988), p. 24.

45   *Ibid.*

46   *Ibid.*

47   Neeson, Eoin, *The Civil War in Ireland 1922–23* (1966), p. 25.

48   *Ibid.*

49   Neeson, Eoin, *The Civil War in Ireland* (1966), p. 26.

50   Hopkinson, Michael, *Green Against Green* (1988), p. 25.

51   Regan, J.M., *The Irish Counter-revolution* (1999), p. 14.

52   *Ibid.*, p. 16.

53   Younger, Calton, *Ireland's Civil War* (1968), p. 154.

54   O'Connor, Frank, *The Big Fellow* (1968), p. 132

55   Younger, Calton, *Ireland's Civil War* (1968), p. 156.

56   *Ibid.*

57   *Ibid.*, p. 158.

58   Hopkinson, Michael, *Green Against Green* (1988), p. 25.

59   Lee, J.J., *Ireland 1912–1985* (1989), p. 49.

60   Lawlor, Sheila, *Britain and Ireland* (1983), p. 111.

61   Regan, J.M., *The Irish Counter-revolution* (1999), p. 11.

62   *Cork Examiner*, 18 Oct. 1921. Newtown is also known as Newtownshandrum.

63   Curran, J.M., *The Birth of the Irish Free State* (1980), p. 115.

64   *Ibid.*

65   Hopkinson, Michael, *Green Against Green* (1988), p. 30.

66   *Ibid.*

67   *Ibid.*

68   Hopkinson, Michael, *Green Against Green* (1988), p. 30.

69   *Ibid.*

70   Curran, J.M., *The Birth of the Irish Free State* (1980), p. 119.

71   *Ibid.*

72   Younger, Calton, *Ireland's Civil War* (1968), p. 185.

73   Curran, J.M., *The Birth of the Irish Free State* (1980), p. 119.

74   Younger, Calton, *Ireland's Civil War* (1968), p. 201.

75   Curran, J.M., *The Birth of the Irish Free State* (1980), p. 120.

76   Regan, J.M., *The Irish Counter-revolution* (1999), p. 20.

77   *Ibid.*, p. 24.

78   *Ibid.*

79   Regan, J.M., *The Irish Counter-revolution* (1999), p. 25.

80   Younger, Calton, *Ireland's Civil War* (1968), p. 185.

81   Regan, J.M., *The Irish Counter-revolution* (1999), p. 16.

82   Younger, Calton, *Ireland's Civil War* (1968), p. 185.
83   Regan, J.M., *The Irish Counter-revolution* (1999), p. 21.
84   Curran, J.M., *The Birth of the Irish Free State* (1980), p. 126.
85   *Ibid.*, p. 124.
86   *Ibid.*
87   *Ibid.*
88   *Ibid.*, p. 128.
89   Curran, J.M., *The Birth of the Irish Free State* (1980), p. 130.
90   Regan, J.M., *The Irish Counter-revolution* (1999), p. 21.
91   Younger, Calton, *Ireland's Civil War* (1968), p. 197.
92   Hopkinson, Michael, *Green Against Green* (1988), p. 34.
93   Regan, J.M., *The Irish Counter-revolution* (1999), p. 23.
94   Younger, Calton, *Ireland's Civil War* (1968), p. 197.
95   Regan, J.M., *The Irish Counter-revolution* (1999), p. 15.
96   Coogan, Tim Pat, *Michael Collins* (1990), p. 295.
97   Lawlor, Sheila, *Britain and Ireland* (1983), p. 147.
98   Coogan, Tim Pat, *Michael Collins* (1990), p. 296.
99   Hopkinson, Michael, *Green Against Green* (1988), p. 35.
100   Curran, J.M., *The Birth of the Irish Free State* (1980), p. 140.
101   Younger, Calton, *Ireland's Civil War* (1968), p. 198.
102   Hopkinson, Michael, *Green Against Green* (1988), p. 39.
103   Regan, J.M., *The Irish Counter-revolution* (1999), p. 15.
104   Lawlor, Sheila, *Britain and Ireland* (1983), p. 147.
105   *Ibid.*
106   Hopkinson, Michael, *Green Against Green* (1988), p. 25.
107   Lawlor, Sheila, *Britain and Ireland* (1983), p. 148.
108   Younger, Calton, *Ireland's Civil War* (1968), p. 200.
109   *Ibid.*
110   Hopkinson, Michael, *Green Against Green* (1988), p. 38.
111   *Ibid.*
112   Lee, J.J., *Ireland 1912–1985* (1989), p. 49.
113   Regan, J.M., *The Irish Counter-revolution* (1999), p. 15.
114   Hopkinson, Michael, *Green Against Green* (1988), p. 39.
115   Younger, Calton, *Ireland's Civil War* (1968), p. 200.
116   Hopkinson, Michael, *Green Against Green* (1988), p. 27.

117 Coogan, Tim Pat, *Michael Collins* (1990), p. 300.

118 Kissane, Bill, *The Politics of the Irish Civil War* (2005), p. 66.

119 Regan, J.M., *The Irish Counter-revolution* (1999), p. 42.

120 Regan, J.M., *The Irish Counter-revolution* (1999), p. 42.

121 Lawlor, Sheila, *Britain and Ireland* (1983), p. 151.

122 Lee, J.J., *Ireland 1912–1985* (1989), p. 50.

123 Younger, Calton, *Ireland's Civil War* (1968), p. 197.

124 *Ibid.*, p. 240.

125 Lee, J.J., *Ireland 1912–1985* (1989), p. 57.

126 Lawlor, Sheila, *Britain and Ireland* (1983), p. 151.

127 Kissane, Bill, *The Politics of the Irish Civil War* (2005) p. 67.

128 O'Donoghue, Florence, *No Other Law* (1986), p. 18.

129 Lee, J.J., *Ireland 1912–1985* (1989), p. 58.

130 Younger, Calton, *Ireland's Civil War* (1968), p. 240.

131 Coogan, Tim Pat, *Michael Collins* (1990), p. 300.

132 *Ibid.*

133 Curran, J.M., *The Birth of the Irish Free State* (1980), p. 175.

134 O'Hegarty, P.S., *The Victory of Sinn Féin* (1998), p. xiii.

135 Kissane, Bill, *The Politics of the Irish Civil War* (2005), p. 65.

136 Hopkinson, Michael, *Green Against Green* (1988), p. 71.

137 *Ibid.*

138 *Ibid.*

139 Hopkinson, Michael, *Green Against Green* (1988), p. 70.

140 Lyons, F.S.L., *Ireland Since the Famine* (1973), p. 456.

141 Regan, J.M., *The Irish Counter-revolution* (1999), p.55.

142 Lyons, F.S.L., *Ireland Since the Famine* (1973), p. 457.

143 Regan, J.M., *The Irish Counter-revolution* (1999), p. 55.

144 Lee, J.J., *Ireland 1912–1985* (1989), p. 58.

145 Regan, J.M., *The Irish Counter-revolution* (1999), p. 59.

146 *Ibid.*

147 Lee, J.J., *Ireland 1912–1985* (1989), p. 58.

148 Curran, J.M., *The Birth of the Irish Free State* (1980), p. 188.

149 Lawlor, Sheila, *Britain and Ireland* (1983), p. 194.

150 *Ibid.*

151 *Ibid.*, p. 151.

152   *Ibid.*, p. 194.

153   Hopkinson, Michael, *Green Against Green* (1988), p. 70.

154   Kissane, Bill, *The Politics of the Irish Civil War* (2005), p. 217.

155   Curran, J.M., *The Birth of the Irish Free State* (1980), p. 222.

156   Hopkinson, Michael, *Green Against Green* (1988), p. 70.

157   *Ibid.*, p. 68.

158   *Ibid.*, p. 73.

159   *Ibid.*, p. 90.

160   *Ibid.*, p. 111.

161   Neeson, Eoin, *The Civil War in Ireland* (1966), p. 123.

162   Hopkinson, Michael, *Green Against Green* (1988), p. 124.

163   *Ibid.*

164   Younger, Calton, *Ireland's Civil War* (1968), p. 342.

165   Hopkinson, Michael, *Green Against Green* (1988), p. 142.

166   Neeson, Eoin, *The Civil War in Ireland* (1966) p. 133.

167   *Ibid.*, p. 134.

168   Younger, Calton, *Ireland's Civil War* (1968), p. 342.

169   Neeson, Eoin, *The Civil War in Ireland* (1966), p. 136.

170   Hopkinson, Michael, *Green Against Green* (1988), p. 144.

171   *Ibid.*

Chapter 2: The Attack on the 'Republic of Munster'

1   Younger, Calton, *Ireland's Civil War* (1968), p. 370.

2   Neeson, Eoin, *The Civil War in Ireland* (1966), p. 161.

3   *Ibid.*

4   Hopkinson, Michael, *Green Against Green* (1988), p. 146.

5   *Ibid.*

6   Neeson, Eoin, *The Civil War in Ireland* (1966), p. 140.

7   *Ibid.*

8   Hopkinson, Michael, *Green Against Green* (1988), p. 147.

9   Younger, Calton, *Ireland's Civil War* (1968), p. 371.

10   M/A, A/0991/3 captured documents lot 3, Coppeen papers, Operations.

11   Neeson, Eoin, *The Civil War in Ireland* (1966), p. 141–2.

12   *Ibid.*, p. 143.

13   *Ibid.*, p. 149.

14   Younger, Calton, *Ireland's Civil War* (1968), p. 377–8.

15   Neeson, Eoin, *The Civil War in Ireland* (1966), p. 145.

16   M/A, A/0991/3 captured documents lot 3, Coppeen papers, Operations.

17   *Cork Examiner*, 17 July 1922.

18   Neeson, Eoin, *The Civil War in Ireland* (1966), p. 146.

19   Hopkinson, Michael, *Green Against Green* (1988), p. 149.

20   Neeson, Eoin, *The Civil War in Ireland* (1966), p. 146.

21   *Ibid.*, p. 148; *Freeman's Journal* 22 July.

22   Younger, Calton, *Ireland's Civil War* (1968), p. 382.

23   Hopkinson, Michael, *Green Against Green* (1988), p. 150.

24   Neeson, Eoin, *The Civil War in Ireland* (1966), p. 149.

25   *Ibid.*, pp. 200–1.

26   *Cork Examiner*, 16 July 1922.

27   Richard Mulcahy papers, UCD, P7/B/21.

28   M/A, A/0991/3 captured documents lot 3, Coppeen papers, Operations.

29   Hopkinson, Michael, *Green Against Green* (1988), p. 150.

30   Neeson, Eoin, *The Civil War in Ireland* (1966), p. 201.

31   Hopkinson, Michael, *Green Against Green* (1988), p. 151.

32   *Ibid.*

33   Younger, Calton, *Ireland's Civil War* (1968), p. 403.

34   South-Western Command daily report, 4 Aug. 1922, Richard Mulcahy papers, P7/B/39.

35   Neeson, Eoin, *The Civil War in Ireland* (1966), p. 203.

36   Siobhán Lankford papers, CAI, U169B, folder 2.

37   *Cork Examiner*, 27 July 1922; Republican Army Official Bulletin.

38   *Freeman's Journal*, 25 July 1922.

39   Ernie O'Malley papers, UCD, P17a/87.

40   Neeson, Eoin, *The Civil War in Ireland* (1966), p. 203.

41   *Ibid.*, p. 204.

42 *Cork Examiner*, 31 July 1922.

43 Ernie O'Malley papers, UCD, P17a/87.

44 *Ibid.*

45 *Freeman's Journal*, 31 July 1922.

46 Neeson, Eoin, *The Civil War in Ireland* (1966), p. 205.

47 *Freeman's Journal*, 3 Aug. 1922.

48 Ernie O'Malley papers, UCD, P17a/87.

49 Neeson, Eoin, *The Civil War in Ireland* (1966), p. 205.

50 *Ibid.*

51 Ernie O'Malley papers, UCD, P17a/87.

52 Richard Mulcahy papers, UCD, P7/B/68.

53 Ernie O'Malley papers, UCD, P17a/87.

54 Neeson, Eoin, *The Civil War in Ireland* (1966), p. 207.

55 Younger, Calton, *Ireland's Civil War* (1968), p. 405.

56 Richard Mulcahy papers, UCD, P7/B/68.

57 *Ibid.*

58 *Ibid.*

59 Narrative of Kilmallock operations, Richard Mulcahy papers, UCD, P7/B/68.

60 *Ibid.*

61 *Ibid.*

62 *Ibid.*

63 *Ibid.*

64 Neeson, Eoin, *The Civil War in Ireland* (1966), p. 209.

65 *Freeman's Journal*, 7 July 1922.

66 Neeson, Eoin, *The Civil War in Ireland* (1966), p. 209.

67 Younger, Calton, *Ireland's Civil War* (1968), p. 406.

Chapter 3: Retreat from Kilmallock

1 O'Donoghue, Florence, *No Other Law* (1986), p. 266.

2 Hopkinson, Michael, *Green Against Green* (1988), p. 155.

3 *Ibid.*, p. 154.

4 *Ibid.*, p. 155.

5 O'Donoghue, Florence, *No Other Law* (1986), pp. 266–7.

6   *Ibid.*, p. 266.

7   *Freeman's Journal*, 15 Aug. 1922.

8   *Ibid.*

9   Younger, Calton, *Ireland's Civil War* (1968), pp. 408–23.

10 Hopkinson, Michael, *Green Against Green* (1988), p. 164.

11 *Ibid.*

12 *Ibid.*

13 *Freeman's Journal*, 8 Aug. 1922.

14 Hopkinson, Michael, *Green Against Green* (1988), p. 152.

15 *Freeman's Journal*, 7 Aug. 1922.

16 *Cork Examiner*, 25 Aug. 1923.

17 *Freeman's Journal*, 15 Aug. 1922.

18 Richard Mulcahy papers, UCD, P7/B/39.

19 Richard Mulcahy papers, UCD, P7/B/113.

20 *Ibid.*

21 Richard Mulcahy papers, UCD, P7/B/39.

22 *Ibid.*

23 M/A, A/0991/3.

24 Richard Mulcahy papers, UCD, P7/B/113.

25 O'Donoghue, Florence, *No Other Law* (1986), p. 267.

26 *Freeman's Journal*, 17 Aug. 1922.

27 *Ibid.*, 17 & 18 Aug. 1922.

28 Ernie O'Malley papers, UCD, P17a/87.

29 Ernie O'Malley papers, UCD, P17a/87.

30 O'Donoghue, Florence, *No Other Law* (1986), p. 268.

31 Ernie O'Malley papers, UCD, P17a/87.

32 Richard Mulcahy papers, UCD, P7/B/93.

33 O'Donoghue, Florence, *No Other Law* (1986), p. 267.

34 Richard Mulcahy papers, UCD, P7/B/93.

35 O'Donoghue, Florence, *No Other Law* (1986), p. 266.

36 Hopkinson, Michael, *Green Against Green* (1988), pp. 164–65.

37 *Ibid.*, p. 172.

38 Hopkinson, Michael, *Green Against Green* (1988), p. 266.

39 *Ibid.*, p. 35.

40 O'Donoghue, Florence, *No Other Law* (1986), p. 268.

41 O'Malley notebooks, UCD, P17b/108.

42 Richard Mulcahy papers, UCD, P7/B/93.

43 O'Donoghue, Florence, *No Other Law* (1986), p. 266.

44 *Ibid.*, p. 297.

45 Richard Mulcahy papers, UCD, P7/B/71.

46 O'Donoghue, Florence, *No Other Law* (1986), p. 267.

47 Hopkinson, Michael, *Green Against Green* (1988), p. 165.

48 O'Donoghue, Florence, *No Other Law* (1986), p. 267.

49 Hopkinson, Michael, *Green Against Green* (1988), p. 175.

50 Richard Mulcahy papers, UCD, P7a/81.

51 Hopkinson, Michael, *Green Against Green* (1988), p. 175.

52 M/A, A/0991/3.

53 Richard Mulcahy papers, UCD, P7/B/71.

54 Richard Mulcahy papers, UCD, P7/B/113.

55 M/A, A/0991/3.

56 *Ibid.*

57 *Ibid.*

58 *Freeman's Journal*, 23 Aug. 1922.

59 M/A, A/0991/3.

60 Richard Mulcahy papers, UCD, P7/B/113.

61 *Ibid.*

62 *Cork Examiner*, 30 Aug. 1922.

63 *Ibid.*

64 M/A, A/0991/3.

65 Richard Mulcahy papers, UCD, P7/B/113.

66 Hopkinson, Michael, *Green Against Green* (1988), pp. 164–5.

67 M/A, A/0991/3.

68 *Ibid.*

69 *Cork Examiner*, 2 Oct. 1922.

70 Ernie O'Malley papers, UCD, P17a/98.

71 Hopkinson, Michael, *Green Against Green* (1988), p. 173.

72 O'Farrell, Peter, *Memoirs of Irish Volunteer activity, 1917–24.*

73 *Ibid.*

74 M/A, A/0991/3.

75   *Cork Examiner*, 12 Sept. 1922.

76   Collated from Ernie O'Malley papers, UCD, P17a/97.

77   Ernie O'Malley papers, UCD, P17a/97.

78   *Cork Examiner*, 31 Aug. 1922.

79   M/A, A/0991/3.

80   *Cork Examiner*, 19 Sept. 1922.

81   *Ibid.*, 22, 24 & 30 Sept. 1922.

82   Ernie O'Malley papers, UCD, P17a/98.

83   *Cork Examiner*, 7 Oct. 1922.

84   Ernie O'Malley papers, UCD, P17a/98.

85   *Cork Examiner*, 11 Oct. 1922.

86   *Ibid.*, 20 Oct. 1922.

87   *Ibid.*

88   Ernie O'Malley papers, UCD, P17a/87; Motherway papers, Michael Byrnes, Charleville.

89   *Cork Examiner*, 27 Oct. 1922.

90   *Cork Examiner*, 1 Nov. 1922.

91   M/A, A/0991/3.

92   Hopkinson, Michael, *Green Against Green* (1988), p. 173.

93   *Irish Times*, 20 Sept. 1922, quoted in Hopkinson, p. 173.

94   Hopkinson, Michael, *Green Against Green* (1988), p. 201.

95   *Ibid.*

96   *Ibid.* p. 202.

97   *Ibid.* p. 162.

98   *Ibid.*

99   *Ibid.* p. 174.

100   Hopkinson, Michael, *Green Against Green* (1988), p. 202.

101   CAI U169B, folder 5, files 6–9.

102   CAI U169 A & B, box 1, file (ii).

103   *Ibid.*

Chapter 4: Difficulties for Republicans

1   Neeson, Eoin, *The Civil War in Ireland* (1966), p. 249.

2   *Ibid.*, p. 251.

3   Younger, Calton, *Ireland's Civil War* (1968), p. 476.

4   Neeson, Eoin, *The Civil War in Ireland* (1966), p. 250.

5   Siobhán Lankford papers, CAI, U169B, folder 5.

6   *Ibid.*

7   Neeson, Eoin, *The Civil War in Ireland* (1966), p. 251.

8   Younger, Calton, *Ireland's Civil War* (1968), p. 476.

9   Hopkinson, Michael, *Green Against Green* (1988), p. 174.

10 *Ibid.*, p. 202.

11 Neeson, Eoin, *The Civil War in Ireland* (1966), p. 251.

12 *Ibid.*

13 *Cork Examiner*, 7 Nov. 1922.

14 *Ibid.*, 10 Nov. 1922.

15 *Ibid.*

16 Michael Shine, 'The Shooting of Molly Egan' (pers. comm.).

17 *Cork Examiner*, 21 Nov. 1922.

18 *Ibid.*

19 *Ibid.*, 17 Nov. 1922.

20 *Ibid.*

21 *Ibid.*

22 Motherway papers, Michael Byrnes, Charleville.

23 Siobhán Lankford papers, CAI, U169, folder 4.

24 *Cork Examiner*, 18 Nov. 1922.

25 Siobhán Lankford papers, CAI, U169 A & B, box 1 (ii).

26 *Cork Examiner*, 29 Nov. 1922.

27 Siobhán Lankford papers, CAI, U169 A & B, box 1 (ii).

28 Younger, Calton, *Ireland's Civil War* (1968), p. 479.

29 *Ibid.*, p. 477.

30 Neeson, Eoin, *The Civil War in Ireland* (1966), p. 273.

31 Younger, Calton, *Ireland's Civil War* (1968), p. 485.

32 Siobhán Lankford papers, CAI, U169 A & B, box 1 (ii).

33 Hopkinson, Michael, *Green Against Green* (1988), p. 189.

34 Siobhán Lankford papers, CAI, U169 A & B, box 1 (ii).

35 Hopkinson, Michael, *Green Against Green* (1988), p. 189.

36 Neeson, Eoin, *The Civil War in Ireland* (1966), pp. 276–7.

37 Richard Mulcahy papers, UCD, P7a/83.

38 M/A, Lot No. 231 file A/1221.

39 Siobhán Lankford papers, CAI, U169, folder 4, file 4/36.

40 Hopkinson, Michael, *Green Against Green* (1988), p. 190.

41 *Ibid.*, p. 191.

42 Neeson, Eoin, *The Civil War in Ireland* (1966), p. 277.

43 Siobhán Lankford papers, CAI, U169 B.

44 *Ibid.*

45 Hopkinson, Michael, *Green Against Green* (1988), p. 192.

46 *Cork Examiner*, 6, 7 Dec. 1922.

47 *Ibid.*, 8 Dec. 1922.

48 *Ibid.*, 14 Dec. 1922.

49 O'Farrell, Peter, *Memoirs of Irish Volunteer activity, 1917–24.*

50 *Cork Examiner*, 19 & 21 Dec. 1922.

51 *Ibid.*, 27 Dec. 1922.

52 *Cork Examiner*, 6 Jan. 1923.

53 M/A, CW/OPS/2/D.

54 *Cork Examiner*, 8 Jan. 1923.

55 Siobhán Lankford papers, CAI, U169 B, folder 4.

56 *Cork Examiner*, 8 Jan. 1923.

57 *Cork Examiner*, 19 Jan. 1923.

58 M/A, CW/OPS/2/D.

Chapter 5: Free State Takes Control.

1 Hopkinson, Michael, *Green Against Green* (1988), p. 228.

2 Neeson, Eoin, *The Civil War in Ireland* (1966), p. 286.

3 O'Donoghue, Florence, *No Other Law* (1986), p. 289.

4 *Ibid.*

5 Hopkinson, Michael, *Green Against Green* (1988), p. 228.

6 Younger, Calton, *Ireland's Civil War* (1968), p. 370.

7 Hopkinson, Michael, *Green Against Green* (1988), p. 228.

8 *Ibid.*

9 O'Donoghue, Florence, *No Other Law* (1986), p. 289.

10 Siobhán Lankford papers, CAI, U169 A & B, box 1 (ii).

11 *Ibid.*

12   Siobhán Lankford papers, CAI, U169 folder 4.

13   *Cork Examiner*, 20 Feb. 1923.

14   Younger, Calton, *Ireland's Civil War* (1968), p. 497.

15   Siobhán Lankford papers, CAI, U169 A & B, box 1 (ii).

16   Younger, Calton, *Ireland's Civil War* (1968), p. 497.

17   Hopkinson, Michael, *Green Against Green* (1988), p. 230.

18   Neeson, Eoin, *The Civil War in Ireland* (1966), p. 286.

19   O'Donoghue, Florence, *No Other Law* (1986), p. 289.

20   Hopkinson, Michael, *Green Against Green* (1988), p. 228.

21   *Cork Examiner*, 9 Feb. 1923.

22   Younger, Calton, *Ireland's Civil War* (1968), p. 497.

23   Neeson, Eoin, *The Civil War in Ireland* (1966), p. 287.

24   O'Donoghue, Florence, *No Other Law* (1986), p. 289.

25   Neeson, Eoin, *The Civil War in Ireland* (1966), p. 287.

26   Hopkinson, Michael, *Green Against Green* (1988), p. 231.

27   CAI U169 folder 4.

28   *Cork Examiner*, 20 Mar. 1923.

29   Hopkinson, Michael, *Green Against Green* (1988), p. 231.

30   CAI U169 folder 4.

31   CAI U169 folder 4.

32   Hopkinson, Michael, *Green Against Green* (1988), p. 232.

33   *Ibid.*, p. 228.

34   *Cork Examiner*, 9 Feb. 1923.

35   Hopkinson, Michael, *Green Against Green* (1988), p. 229.

36   Siobhán Lankford papers, CAI, U169 B, box 2, folder 5.

37   *Cork Examiner*, 12 Feb. 1923.

38   Hopkinson, Michael, *Green Against Green* (1988), p. 232.

39   *Cork Examiner*, 8 Mar. 1923.

40   *Ibid.*, 9 & 12, Feb. 1923.

41   *Ibid.*, 19 Feb. 1923.

42   *Ibid.*, 24 Feb. 1923.

43   Siobhán Lankford papers, CAI, U169 B.

44   *Cork Examiner*, 13 & 17 Feb. 1923.

45   M/A, A/8454.

46   M/A, CW/OPS/2M.

47 M/A, CW/OPS/2/D.

48 M/A, CW/OPS/2/D.

49 M/A, CW/OPS/2M

50 *Ibid.*

51 *Ibid.*

52 Neeson, Eoin, *The Civil War in Ireland* (1966), p. 243.

53 M/A, CW/OPS/District and Officer.

54 *Ibid.*

55 Neeson, Eoin, *The Civil War in Ireland* (1966), p. 251.

56 O'Farrell, Peter, *Memoirs of Irish Volunteer activity, 1917–24.*

57 Collated from documents in M/A, CW/OPS/2/M.

58 Siobhán Lankford papers, CAI, B, folder 4.

59 *Ibid.*

60 Hopkinson, Michael, *Green Against Green* (1988), p. 240.

61 *Ibid.*

62 *Ibid.*, p. 239.

63 O'Donoghue, Florence, *No Other Law* (1986), p. 298.

64 *Ibid.*, p. 233.

65 *Ibid.*

66 O'Donoghue, Florence, *No Other Law* (1986), p. 298.

67 Hopkinson, Michael, *Green Against Green* (1988), p. 237.

68 *Ibid.*

69 O'Donoghue, Florence, *No Other Law* (1986), p. 301.

70 Hopkinson, Michael, *Green Against Green* (1988), p. 238.

71 O'Donoghue, Florence, *No Other Law* (1986), p. 303.

72 Hopkinson, Michael, *Green Against Green* (1988), p. 238.

73 O'Donoghue, Florence, *No Other Law* (1986), p. 305.

74 Hopkinson, Michael, *Green Against Green* (1988), p. 238.

75 Younger, Calton, *Ireland's Civil War* (1968), p. 507.

76 *Ibid.*, p. 508.

77 Siobhán Lankford papers, CAI, U169 B (iv).

78 Younger, Calton, *Ireland's Civil War* (1968), p. 509.

Chapter 6: Conclusion

1 M/A, CW/OPS/3/B.

2   M/A, CW/OPS/2/4.

3   M/A, CW/OPS/3/B.

4   *Ibid.*

5   Hopkinson, Michael, *Green Against Green* (1988), p. 272.

6   *Ibid.*

7   Younger, Calton, *Ireland's Civil War* (1968), p. 517.

8   *Ibid.*, p. 512.

Appendix

1   Townshend, Charles, *Easter 1916: The Irish Rebellion* (2005).

2   O'Donoghue, Florence, *No Other Law* (1986).

3   Hopkinson, Michael, *Green Against Green* (1988).

4   O'Donoghue, Florence, *No Other Law* (1986).

5   Borgonovo, John (ed.), *Florence and Josephine O'Donoghue's War of Independence* (2006).

6   Jones, Thomas (ed. Keith Middlemas), *Whitehall Diary, Volume 3: Ireland 1918–1925* (1971).

7   Hopkinson, Michael, *Green Against Green* (1988).

8   Breen, Dan, *My Fight for Irish Freedom* (1981).

9   Jones, Thomas (ed. Keith Middlemas), *Whitehall Diary*, (1971).

10   Borgonovo, John (ed.), *Florence and Josephine O'Donoghue's War of Independence* (2006).

11   Jones, Thomas (ed. Keith Middlemas), *Whitehall Diary*, (1971).

12   Borgonovo, John (ed.), *Florence and Josephine O'Donoghue's War of Independence* (2006).

13   Witness statement, Comdt Paddy O'Brien, Bureau of Military History.

14   Jones, Thomas (ed. Keith Middlemas), *Whitehall Diary*, (1971).

15   Borgonovo, John (ed.), *Florence and Josephine O'Donoghue's War of Independence* (2006).

16   *Ibid.*

17   Jones, Thomas (ed. Keith Middlemas), *Whitehall Diary*, (1971).

18   Younger, Calton, *Ireland's Civil War* (1968).

19   Jones, Thomas (ed. Keith Middlemas), *Whitehall Diary*, (1971).

20   Borgonovo, John (ed.), *Florence and Josephine O'Donoghue's War of Independence* (2006).

21   *Ibid.*

22   Kissane, Bill, *The Politics of the Irish Civil War* (2005).

23   O'Donoghue, Florence, *No Other Law* (1986).

24   Hopkinson, Michael, *Green Against Green* (1988).

25   *Ibid.*

26   Breen, Dan, *My Fight for Irish Freedom* (1981).

27   Hopkinson, Michael, *Green Against Green* (1988).

28   Borgonovo, John (ed.), *Florence and Josephine O'Donoghue's War of Independence* (2006).

29   Jones, Thomas (ed. Keith Middlemas), *Whitehall Diary*, (1971).

30   *Ibid.*

31   Borgonovo, John (ed.), *Florence and Josephine O'Donoghue's War of Independence* (2006).

32   Jones, Thomas (ed. Keith Middlemas), *Whitehall Diary*, (1971).

33   Witness statement 787, Bureau of Military History, Con Meaney.

34   O'Donoghue, Florence, *No Other Law* (1986).

35   *Ibid.*

36   Borgonovo, John (ed.), *Florence and Josephine O'Donoghue's War of Independence* (2006).

37   Hopkinson, Michael, *Green Against Green* (1988).

38   Borgonovo, John (ed.), *Florence and Josephine O'Donoghue's War of Independence* (2006).

39   Witness statement 764, Bureau of Military History, Paddy O'Brien.

40   Jones, Thomas (ed. Keith Middlemas), *Whitehall Diary*, (1971).

41   Borgonovo, John (ed.), *Florence and Josephine O'Donoghue's War of Independence* (2006).

42   Hopkinson, Michael, *Green Against Green* (1988).

43   O'Farrell, Peter, *Memoirs of Irish Volunteer activity, 1917–24.*

44   Borgonovo, John (ed.), *Florence and Josephine O'Donoghue's War of Independence* (2006).

45   *Ibid.*

46   O'Donoghue, Florence, *No Other Law* (1986).

47   Hopkinson, Michael, *Green Against Green* (1988).

48   *Ibid.*

49   O'Donoghue, Florence, *No Other Law* (1986).

50   Jones, Thomas (ed. Keith Middlemas), *Whitehall Diary*, (1971).

51   Neeson, Eoin, *The Civil War in Ireland* (1966).

Bibliography

Primary Sources

Cork

Cork Archives Institute, minute books of Charleville Rural District Council

Cork Archives Institute, Siobhán Lankford papers, box 1, U169B

Cork Archives Institute, Siobhán Lankford papers, box 2, U169B

Cork City Library, *Cork Examiner*, microfilm

Cork City Library, *Irish Times*, microfilm

University College, Cork, RIC County Cork inspectors' reports, microfilm

Dublin

Military Archives, CW/OPS, Limerick Command

Military Archives, CW/OPS, Cork Command

Military Archives, document no. WS 764, Commandant Paddy O'Brien, O/C Cork No. 4 Brigade

Military Archives, document no. WS 754, Michael Geary, Company O/C Charleville and Richard Smith, assistant battalion adjutant Charleville, 3rd Battalion, Cork No. 4 Brigade

Military Archives, document no. WS 1,027, Michael Motherway, member of Irish Volunteers, Charleville

Military Archives, document no. WS 64 and 787, Con Meaney, O/C 7th Battalion, Cork No. 2 Brigade and later O/C 1st Battalion Cork No. 4 Brigade

O'Malley, Ernie, papers, UCD
O'Malley, Ernie, notebooks, UCD
Mulcahy, Richard, papers, UCD

NEWSPAPERS

Cork Examiner
Irish Times
Limerick Leader
Freeman's Journal

BOOKS

Aubane Historical Society, *Seán Moylan in His Own Words* (Aubane Historical Society, 2004)

Augusteijn, Joost, *From Public Defiance to Guerilla Warfare* (Amsterdam, 1994)

Borgonovo, John (ed.), *Florence and Josephine O'Donoghue's War of Independence* (Dublin: Irish Academic Press, 2006)

Breen, Dan, *My Fight for Irish Freedom* (Tralee: Anvil Books, 1981)

Coogan, Tim Pat, *Michael Collins* (London: Hutchinson, 1990)

Curran, J.M., *The Birth of the Irish Free State: 1921–1923* (Alabama: Alabama University Press, 1980)

Deasy, Liam, *Brother Against Brother* (Cork: Mercier Press, 1982)

Farry, Michael, *The Aftermath of Revolution, Sligo 1921–23* (Dublin: University College Dublin Press, 2000)

Fitzpatrick, David, *Politics and Irish Life 1919–1921: Provincial Experience of War and Revolution* (Cork: Cork University Press, 1998)

Garvin, Tom, *The Evolution of Irish Nationalist Politics* (Dublin: Gill & Macmillan, 1981)

Garvin Tom, *Nationalist Revolutionaries in Ireland 1858–1928* (Oxford: Clarendon Press, 1987)

Garvin, Tom, *1922: The Birth of Irish Democracy* (Dublin: Gill & Macmillan, 2005)

Hart, Peter, *The I.R.A. and its Enemies* (Oxford: Clarendon Press, 1998)

Hart, Peter, *The I.R.A. at War* (Oxford: Oxford University Press, 2003)

Herlihy, Jim, *The Royal Irish Constabulary: A Short History and Genealogical Guide* (Dublin: Four Courts Press, 1997)

Hopkinson, Michael, *Green Against Green* (Dublin: Gill & Macmillan, 1988)

Jones, Thomas (ed. Keith Middlemas), *Whitehall Diary, Volume 3: Ireland 1918–1925* (London: Oxford University Press, 1971)

Kissane, Bill, *The Politics of the Irish Civil War* (Oxford: Oxford University Press, 2005)

Laffan, Michael, *The Resurrection of Ireland: The Sinn Féin Party, 1916–1923* (New York: Cambridge University Press, 1999)

Lawlor, Sheila, *Britain and Ireland 1914–23* (Dublin: Gill & Macmillan, 1983)

Lee, J.J., *Ireland 1912–1985: Politics and Society* (Cambridge: Cambridge University Press, 1989)

Meagher, Jim, *The War of Independence in North Cork 1913–22* (Charleville and District Historical Society, 2004)

Neeson, Eoin, *The Civil War in Ireland 1922–23* (Cork: Mercier Press, 1966)

O'Connor, Frank, *The Big Fellow. Michael Collins and the Irish Revolution* (Dublin: Clonmore & Reynolds, 1965)

O'Donoghue, Florence, *No Other Law* (Dublin: Anvil Books, 1986)

O'Farrell, Peter, *Memoirs of Irish Volunteer activity, 1917–24* (unpublished)

O'Hegarty, P.S., *The Victory of Sinn Féin* (Dublin: UCD Press, 1998)

O'Malley, Ernie, *The Singing Flame* (Anvil, Dublin, 1978)

Purdon, Edward, *The Civil War* (Cork: Mercier Press, 2000)

Regan, John M., *The Irish Counter-revolution 1921–1936: Treaty-ite Politics and Settlement in Independent Ireland* (Dublin: Gill & Macmillan, 1999)

Ryan, Meda, *Liam Lynch: The Real Chief* (Cork: Mercier Press, 1986)

Townshend, Charles, *Easter 1916: The Irish Rebellion* (London: The Penguin Group, 2005)

Townshend, Charles, *The British Campaign in Ireland* (London: Oxford University Press, 1975)

Valiulis, M.G., *Portrait of a Revolutionary: General Richard Mulc-ahy and the Founding of the Irish Free State* (Dublin: Irish Academic Press, Dublin, 1992)

White, Gerry and O'Shea, Brendan, *Baptised in Blood: The Formation of the Cork Brigade of the Irish Volunteers 1913–1916* (Cork: Mercier Press, 2005)

Younger, Calton, *Ireland's Civil War* (London: Muller, 1968)

Index

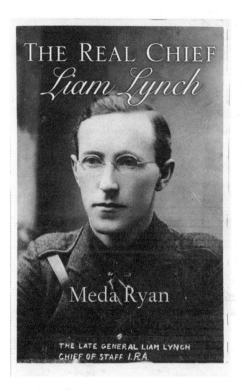

The Real Chief: Liam Lynch

Meda Ryan

With the aid of Liam Lynch's personal letters, private documents and historical records, *The Real Chief* traces the turbulent career of one of Ireland's greatest guerrilla commanders from his birth in 1893 until his death twenty-nine years later in the Civil War, when he was killed in action in the Knockmealdown Mountains.

ISBN: 978 1 85635 460 8